Rescued

A True Story of Enduring Love

Yolanda
&
Tom Barbagallo

REDEMPTION
PRESS

Rescued

Contents

Acknowledgments

$\mathcal{W}$ RITING THIS BOOK was a joint effort with Tom, my dear husband, co-author, and best friend. I'm deeply indebted to him for his extensive help in writing along with me. I couldn't have done this project without him.

A very special thanks to our daughter Karen for her hard work and dedication. As a busy mom of twin boys, she patiently typed our handwritten pages, numerous revisions, and everything necessary for submission to the publisher. We greatly appreciate the endless hours she spent on the computer and her suggestions to improve the manuscript.

Lancaster Christian Writers, a group we belong to, played a significant role in providing input to make our story come alive. The monthly meetings with critique groups and periodic seminars and workshops helped us enormously. A special thanks to fellow writers for going the extra mile to influence us in a positive and inspiring way.

A big thank you to our friends at church for continued prayers since the inception of this project. Your love, kind words, and encouragement also played a valuable part in helping us stay focused until we finished writing.

Thanks to our daughter Michele and our dear relatives and friends who have waited patiently for this book to be published. Your love and support have meant a lot to us.

We are very grateful to the publishing team who made our book a reality. Thank you very much.

Chapter 1

Locked Up

$\mathcal{A}$ TWENTY-SIX-YEAR-OLD WOMAN, married only three weeks, I found myself behind bars in southern Vermont. I felt isolated that day in September 1969, because of being locked up and cut off from the outside world. Loneliness and fear welled up within me. How devastating to be separated from Tom, without any idea what would happen to me next. I almost felt as if I were suffocating because of the thick air of tension that filled the jail atmosphere. Just breathing air into my lungs became a struggle. My body ached all over.

The jail cell was a poorly-lit, dreary room with a strong odor of mildew. It looked about twenty by thirty feet. It had only a cot to sleep on and a metal folding chair. There were no windows. A commode and sink filled one corner of the cell.

As I stood in the cell and looked around, I was horrified to see at least a dozen large, black spiders around the edge of the floor and on the walls near the ceiling. I wanted to scream out for help, but I knew it wouldn't do any good. There was no one in the jail but me.

I felt paralyzed with fear after seeing the spiders. *God, help me,* I thought. *I'm feeling so lightheaded. My knees are going to buckle at any moment. I'm going to pass out. I think I may throw up.*

I gripped the back of the metal chair to steady myself and started breaking out in a cold sweat, with perspiration and chills coming over me.

1

I missed Tom so much and wished he could hold me close and comfort me. In the past, whenever I saw a spider near me, I'd scream and he'd come to my rescue and kill it. I could barely muster up the strength to move the cot and chair away from the wall to the center of the room. *I have to get as far away as possible from all these ugly, creepy spiders. The thought of them crawling on me while I sleep frightens me to death.*

I had a pounding headache and felt too worn out to do anything more to help myself. I sat down on the cold, hard folding chair, attempting to rest and collect my thoughts. My mind was a blur. *I have no energy left in my body; I just want to collapse and go to sleep.*

By this time, it was about seven o'clock. The last meal I had had that day was a small bowl of cold cereal and milk for breakfast. I don't remember being offered any food after getting arrested. Even though I would normally be starved by this time in the evening, I had no appetite.

I felt exhausted physically, mentally, and emotionally. My head spun. My mind raced. Prior to that day, I had never been in trouble with the law. Little did I know that my life was about to further unravel in ways that were beyond my comprehension.

Earlier that morning, my husband had left for work, excited about his new job assignment at a nuclear power plant construction site. I missed him while he worked and always anticipated his return later in the afternoon. I looked forward to a peaceful day at the motel, where we planned to stay until we could find a place to rent.

The motel had two floors, and we were on the second floor. Inside the front door, a kitchenette with a wall behind it partially divided the front and back of the room. Behind the wall, a closet and bathroom faced a bed at the rear of the room. The front door led to a stairway down to the motel office on the first floor. The back door opened to a stone driveway level with the second floor where we parked our car, a two-door, turquoise 1969 Chevrolet Impala with a black vinyl top. The room didn't have a telephone. If we needed to make a phone call, we had to use a pay phone near the motel office.

Shortly after Tom left, I stepped outside the front door of the motel room to check out the weather. I looked at the sky and countryside and took a few deep breaths of fresh, cool air. *How invigorating,* I thought.

What a beautiful morning. The sun is shining brightly, with patches of thick, fluffy white clouds floating under the deep blue sky. I'll have to get out later and take a walk.

We had gotten married in New York City on a Tuesday, and on Saturday we moved to Vermont.

I still had to work through the crushing stress leading up to getting married. We had eloped four days before our planned wedding date of August 16th. I felt relieved the past turmoil in my life had finally ended. Now I could experience a fresh start. Never would I have imagined I'd be sitting in a jail cell later that day.

A series of unexpected events caused the day to become overwhelming and chaotic. In mid-morning while I sat at the kitchenette table thinking about what to prepare for dinner, it startled me to hear loud knocking on the motel door. I stood up and walked cautiously to the door and asked, "Who is it?"

"I'm the motel owner. I have a special delivery letter for you."

"Could you please slide it under the door?"

After picking up the envelope and sitting down, I held it in my hands and looked at it. I wondered, *How did Mom know where we are staying, since neither Tom nor I told her? More than likely Tom gave his mother the name and address of the motel, and my mom found out from her.*

I felt uneasy about opening the envelope because I suspected the letter would upset me. I slowly tore the envelope open. As I pulled out the letter and started to read it, the energy began draining from my body, and my stomach felt queasy. Tears poured down my cheeks and splashed onto the letter. *I wish Tom was here with me to hold me in his arms.*

Mom rehashed everything that had bothered her leading up to my getting married to Tom. Here we were miles apart, and I was still being reminded of the unpleasant and stressful things I wanted to put behind me. A feeling of deep despair came over me. *How much longer will the tension between Mom and me go on? I love her and want our relationship restored, but I don't know how to make it happen.*

Later that morning, a group of boisterous teenagers rented the room next door. The motel walls were paper-thin, so I could hear loud shouting, high-pitched laughing, and occasional banging on the walls. It sounded as if the rowdy teens were in my room. The disturbing uproar continued nonstop. I made sure the front and back doors were locked. *I'd feel much safer with Tom here.*

A few weeks before we were married, he happened to tell me about two-way mirrors. I remembered Tom saying, "There are mirrors where people can see what is going on in front of a mirror from behind the mirror." Prior to that time, I was unaware of anyone being able to look through the back side of a mirror.

I found it difficult to think straight because of the stress Mom's letter had caused me and all the noise coming from the room next door. As a result, my imagination got the better of me. *Can the teenagers see me through a two-way mirror from their room into my bathroom?*

The bathroom mirror was attached to the wall adjoining our rooms. All I could think to do was to hang two large bath towels over the light fixture to cover the mirror. With the lights on, I carefully draped each towel over the fixture to make sure the mirror was completely concealed. Feeling somewhat relieved after covering the mirror, I left the bathroom and partially closed the bathroom door. I went to the refrigerator to get a cold drink and sat at the kitchenette table to try to calm down.

Within a short time, I smelled smoke coming from the bedroom area. I thought, *Something must be burning.*

When I went to check it out, I saw flames in the bathroom. *Oh, no! What happened? I've got to get help!*

I rushed out the front door of the room, ran over to the stairs and down to the motel office, and told the owner to call the fire department. The firemen got there soon afterwards and put the fire out. Then I heard one of them yell, "Call the police!"

Meanwhile, a fireman had called Tom at work and told him about a fire at the motel and that he needed to come immediately. After he arrived, one of the firemen took him into the room to show him the aftermath of the fire, which I never got to see.

I stood outside the back door of the room with two police officers. *Why aren't the police and firemen asking me what happened?*

When Tom came outside we didn't get to talk, and since everything happened so quickly, I was unable to think clearly. I heard one of the officers say to Tom, "Your wife has to go with us to the police station."

I was completely in a daze at this point. The police walked me to their car, and one of them held open the rear door and asked me politely, "Would you please get in?"

As I got into the vehicle, I felt confused and couldn't comprehend what was going on. *Why am I going to the police station? What crime did I commit? What did the fireman talk to Tom about in the motel room?*

Tom followed the police to town in our car. After we arrived at the police station, the officers took me inside. Tom walked behind us. One of the officers stepped back to talk with Tom and said quietly, "Your wife is going to be charged with arson."

I overheard what he told Tom. *What's going to happen to me? Am I going to jail? Do I have to be separated from Tom? I never even got to talk to him after the fire. My body feels like it's going numb.*

Next, the police took me to a room where they fingerprinted me and took mug shots. Tom was not allowed to come with me. He waited outside the door. Afterwards, I got to see him only a few moments before he left the police station.

Before he left, he said, "I'll find a lawyer for you, Yolanda."

Some time in the afternoon, the same two officers escorted me to their patrol car, and I got in the back seat. After about fifteen minutes of driving, the car slowed down as we entered a much smaller town compared to where the police station was located. The officers pulled up to a building and parked.

They ushered me inside to a jail cell and locked me up. *This whole day is like one big nightmare. I wish I could wake up and it would all be over.*

I was grateful my mom and dad didn't know what had happened to me. It was the last thing I wanted them to find out.

Chapter 2

Return to America

*T*OM AND DAD were of Hungarian descent. Their parents had moved from Hungary to the United States before my parents were born. The two families didn't know one another. Dad was born in 1908 in Pittsburgh, Pennsylvania, and Mom in 1917 in Bridgeport, Connecticut. After Mom and Dad were born, their parents returned to Hungary. My parents didn't live in America long enough to learn English. They grew up on farms and never met one another while living in Hungary.

As I grew up, I enjoyed learning about their lives, both during their time in Hungary and after they came back to America. One day, I questioned Dad while we sat in the living room waiting for Mom to finish preparing dinner. I asked, "What was it like living on a farm in Hungary?"

"I had to get up early in the morning and work hard all day and into the night," he replied with a frown. "I didn't like farming."

"You must have been exhausted working those long hours."

"I was." He looked at me with his penetrating blue eyes and continued, "I wanted to come to the United States and find another kind of work."

I sat on the edge of my chair and asked, "How old were you when you left Hungary and came to this country?"

"Sixteen."

"That's very young to be on your own. I could never imagine leaving my family at such an early age. Where did you live when you got here and what kind of work did you do?"

"I lived with relatives in Pittsburgh, Pennsylvania, and worked at a steel mill."

"Did you like that job?"

"No." He shook his head with a look of disgust. "The place was very hot and dirty and I had to do heavy lifting." Then his eyes lit up. "I moved to New York City and got a job cooking in a restaurant, which I liked much better."

It turned out that cooking became his lifelong career.

When Mom was eight years old, her father died at the age of forty-eight from an infection caused by a farm accident. Her mother was left with five children, ranging in age from one to eighteen.

While Mom and I sat at the kitchen table having lunch one day, she told me, "It was a difficult time for my family after losing my father. I felt very sad and cried a lot because I missed him. He died just before I made my First Holy Communion. It should have been a happy occasion for me, but it wasn't." With her eyes watering, she continued, "To make matters worse, because I was mourning my father's death, I had to wear a black dress for the church ceremony while all the other girls wore beautiful white dresses."

I reached across the table and held Mom's hand gently. "I can't imagine how awful it must have been to lose your father when you were so young and then for you to be dressed in black for your First Holy Communion."

What Mom shared made me realize that she had struggled through hard times as a young girl. In 1933, at the age of sixteen, she left her family and came back to America. In those days, the only means for travel between countries was by sea.

I asked her, "How was the trip?"

"Not good. I was seasick most of the time. I couldn't wait to get off the ship."

"How long did the trip take?"

"Between traveling by train from Hungary to Hamburg, Germany, and then taking a ship from there to America, it took about three weeks."

"I'm sure it must have been a big relief to get here."

"Yes!" She paused and took a deep breath. "As the ship entered New York harbor and I saw the Statue of Liberty, I had tears in my eyes."

"Did you have any relatives in New York?"

"No. My parents had good friends, Mr. and Mrs. Orosz, in Long Island City, New York. They had moved from Hungary to the United States years earlier. I stayed with them temporarily until I could find a job."

"What kind of work did you find?"

"I got a job cooking and housekeeping for a wealthy couple in their home on Fifth Avenue in Manhattan. I lived there while I worked for them."

"Did you and Dad learn any English before you came to this country?"

"No. Our parents spoke only Hungarian to us, and our schooling took place in Hungary. We began to learn English after we came to America."

I wanted to know how my parents met. I asked Mom, "How did you meet Dad?"

"We met at Saint Stephen's of Hungary Catholic Church on 82nd Street in Manhattan, at a dance in the church's social hall," she replied with a sparkle in her eyes.

"Why, Mom, that's the same church we attended as a family when we lived on 65th Street in Manhattan."

She nodded with a smile.

My parents got married at Saint Stephen's Church in 1938. Shortly afterwards, Mom got pregnant. What a happy occasion for my parents when James, their first child, was born. He lived to be only seven months old. One morning while we sat on the couch and chatted, Mom explained what had happened to him.

She said, "I put James in for a nap the same way I did every day. I checked on him later and he seemed to be asleep. As I looked at him more closely, I panicked because I realized he wasn't breathing. I picked him up and desperately tried to wake him, but I couldn't. I called for help, but it was too late." Mom hesitated as her voice cracked and tears trickled down her cheeks. Choked up, she continued, "We could do nothing to revive him. Dad and I were horrified and in shock. We had James for such a short time, and suddenly he was gone."

I had tears in my eyes as she shared what happened. I slid closer to her on the couch and put my arm around her. "Mom, you and Dad must have been devastated."

"Yes, terribly. We were heartbroken. It was painful for us whenever we saw parents with their infants and young children."

"Did you find out what caused his death?"

"Yes. The doctor told us he died from crib death."

Sudden Infant Death Syndrome (SIDS) later became the term used to describe my brother's death. After two miscarriages, Mom got pregnant again and gave birth to me, and later, to my brothers, Al and Jim.

Mom loved spending time in the kitchen. I have wonderful memories of her meals and desserts and the delicious aromas that filled our home. My favorite meals were stuffed peppers, fried chicken, goulash, and stuffed cabbage. One meal I disliked was lentils topped with fried onions, but eventually I developed a taste for it.

I always looked forward to the mouthwatering desserts Mom baked. I have special memories of her delicious peach pies when we lived in Jackson Heights, New York. She used freshly picked, ripe peaches from the two full-grown trees in our backyard. Some of her other scrumptious treats were walnut cake with rum frosting and two Hungarian desserts, palascinta (crepes filled with sweetened cottage cheese and golden raisins), and pogasca (biscuits made with sour cream, butter, and golden raisins).

Neither of my parents smoked, so they were a good example for me. However, during my teen years I hung out with a neighborhood crowd and most of them smoked. I decided to buy a pack of cigarettes after trying a few I got from my friends. They left a bad taste in my mouth, but I did it anyway to go along with them. I smoked only around my friends, but my parents found out and wanted me to quit. Mom's meals didn't taste as flavorful when I smoked. I decided to give it up after realizing my parents' disappointment and noticing its effect on my taste buds.

Mom started working in a sewing factory. Eventually, she quit the job and worked at home doing alterations for numerous customers. She made me pretty dresses. One was a white Holy Communion dress with lace trim. For my high school prom, she sewed a peach-colored dress from silk chiffon.

My parents took turns with our relatives celebrating holidays. I remember it always being a happy and fun time whether at our place or theirs. Typically, one of my uncles started singing Hungarian songs after the meal and everyone else joined in. The song, "Az A Szep," became my favorite. It's a lively and amusing song about a lady who has dark blue eyes but doesn't feel pretty enough for her sweetheart.

Mom and Dad's formal education finished after completing the sixth grade. This was customary in Hungary for children living in farming communities. After coming to America, as much as they might have wanted further education, it wasn't practical for them. They had to find work soon after arriving here. However, they had a strong desire to send their children to college. This meant they had to work and save money to make their dream possible.

Chapter 3

Big Apple

I WAS BORN in 1942 in Brooklyn, New York. My parents and I lived in an apartment on New Jersey Avenue in Brooklyn. Almost three years later, my brother Al was born. Afterwards, we moved to an apartment on East 82nd Street in Manhattan. I attended kindergarten while we lived there. My brother Jim was born after we moved down to East 65th Street. He and I are six years apart in age.

I completed the first through fourth grades at Saint John Nepomucene School. It took me five minutes to walk one block to get there from home. I learned about the Catholic faith using a catechism, which is a handbook of questions and answers for teaching the principles of a religion. Homework assignments included memorizing answers to catechism questions. One in particular I remember is, "Why did God make me?" The answer was, "God made me to know Him, to love Him, and to serve Him."

In addition to his full-time job as a cook, Dad was superintendent of the apartment building where we lived. His responsibilities included taking care of the building and resolving problems tenants brought to his attention. When I was around seven years old, I occasionally watched him shovel coal into a large furnace to provide heat and hot water for tenants. Our apartment had a kitchen, living room, bathroom, and two bedrooms, one for my parents and me, and the other for my brothers.

Next, we moved to Jackson Heights, located in the borough of Queens, which is surrounded by the Bronx, Manhattan, Brooklyn, and Long Island. My parents bought a single-family home about a mile from La Guardia Airport. At first, I heard the deafening noise of planes taking off and landing, but eventually I got used to it and hardly noticed the noise anymore. While living in this home, I attended Saint Gabriel's School and completed the fifth and sixth grades. The school was a ten-minute walk from home.

One day, the secretary called from St. Stephen's of Hungary Church, and I answered the phone. She told me my family had won a television set. What a surprise because we had never had one. I almost dropped the phone in my excitement. I rushed to tell my parents and brothers, and they were just as excited as I was. My parents had bought a number of raffle tickets, and one of theirs got picked. After delivery of the TV, I could hardly believe we actually owned one. It was a black and white TV, enclosed in a dark brown, wooden cabinet that went well with our living room furniture. Just because we had this new form of entertainment, it didn't mean my brothers and I could watch TV all the time. Mom and Dad made a rule that we could only watch it on weekends. They didn't want us to get distracted from doing our homework during the week.

Washing clothes in our household wasn't like it is today with an automatic washer. Mom used an old-fashioned wringer washer. She put each article of clothing through the wringer with one hand and used the other hand to turn the wringer handle at the same time. This squeezed out the excess water after both washing and rinsing clothes.

At the age of five, my brother Jim decided to experiment with the wringer while no one was looking. Mom and I heard something going on in the laundry room, and when we went to check it out, we found Jim with his arm stuck in the wringer up to his elbow. Mom rescued him. Fortunately he wasn't injured. As far as I know, he never tried that stunt again.

When I was ten years old, my maternal grandmother came from Hungary to live with us. Mom took her to the doctor for a checkup because she looked underweight to the point of possibly being unhealthy. He recommended she start taking vitamins every day. Along with the doctor's advice and Mom's great cooking and baking, she soon gained weight and looked much healthier.

Grandma couldn't speak English and never had the desire to learn. She felt content to speak her language with our family, relatives, and Hungarian friends. I learned Hungarian as my first language, which allowed me to communicate well with my grandmother. I taught my friends how to say in Hungarian, "Is Yolanda at home?" When they came over to visit and Grandma opened the door, she could understand what they were saying.

My grandmother raised chickens in the empty lot next to our property, similar to the way she did while living in Hungary on her farm. She kept them in a coop, which is a wire cage used for keeping chickens confined. The coop measured about eight by ten feet and six feet tall and housed approximately a dozen chickens. After enjoying a meal one Sunday, my brothers and I found out we had eaten two of the chickens. We were upset but had to get used to the idea that Grandma raised them to feed us, and that they weren't our pets.

For the seven years she lived with our family, I enjoyed the many conversations we had in Hungarian, which helped us form a close bond. She passed away at the age of seventy-three when I was seventeen. I missed her and still hold dear the memory of having Grandma as a part of our family.

Our final move took us to a new two-family brick house in Rego Park. This location in Queens turned out to be a much quieter neighborhood compared to the one near the airport. The home had an upstairs apartment that my parents rented out.

One Christmas, my parents decided to surprise Jim with a bicycle. After my brothers and I went to bed on Christmas Eve, Mom and Dad stood the bike on its kickstand in front of the seven-foot silver artificial Christmas tree that we set up each year. When we got up the next morning, we were shocked. The bike had fallen over and knocked down the tree. Fortunately, the bike and tree weren't damaged. Of course, Jim was delighted to get the bike and couldn't wait to ride it.

I completed the seventh and eighth grades at Resurrection Ascension School. I commuted by public transportation, taking two city buses, since Queens did not use school buses. How happy I felt to complete my elementary education after attending four different schools from kindergarten through eighth grade. Changing schools had always been an adjustment because I left behind friends and had to make new ones all over again.

From ages ten to thirteen, I enjoyed taking Hungarian folk dancing lessons. My teacher, Aranka, was a kind, patient, and friendly Hungarian lady. I took lessons on Saturdays in Manhattan, along with two of my close friends, Mary Ann and Elaine. We had beautiful costumes to wear for our yearly recitals that were held at the Hungarian church's auditorium. We wore knee-length, full, white skirts with crinoline slips to keep the skirts belled out; a white, short-sleeved peasant blouse with puffy sleeves; and a red vest embroidered with pink, white, and blue flowers attached to green stems and leaves. The skirt had red, white, and green strips of shiny, one-inch ribbon encircling the bottom of the skirt, six inches from the hem. The red, white, and green colors symbolized the Hungarian flag.

At one of our recitals, I danced a duet with my friend Mary Ann. During the performance, I felt embarrassed when my slip started to fall down. I rushed off the stage. My teacher quickly fastened the undergarment, and I ran back onstage. The audience clapped enthusiastically when I made a comeback and again after we finished dancing. The most memorable folk dancing performance for me occurred when our class of about sixteen students appeared on *The Ed Sullivan Show* in the early 1950s. This popular TV variety show broadcasted live from Manhattan on Sunday evenings from eight to nine o'clock.

On occasion during the summer, Dad took my brothers and me to Brighton Beach located in Brooklyn, not far from the well-known amusement park, Coney Island. We took the subway, since my family didn't have a car, and the trip took forty-five minutes. After getting off the train, we stopped at a delicatessen near the beach. Dad ordered bologna sandwiches with mustard. By the time we got to the beach, we were hungry and couldn't wait to lay out our blankets on the hot sand, sit down, and eat our sandwiches. Dad liked to swim, and we learned from him. We spent the day riding the waves and swimming in the ocean. I always enjoyed those fun-filled times with Dad and my brothers.

Mom didn't like the beach, so she stayed home and kept busy cooking and doing household chores. She always had a delicious meal waiting for us after we arrived home. As much as I loved spending the day at the ocean, I looked forward to going home and being with Mom.

I went to an all-girls Catholic high school, Our Lady of Wisdom Academy, in Ozone Park. I commuted by public transportation, taking three buses to get there, which took about fifty minutes each way. What a relief for me to go to the same high school all the way through!

All the girls wore a uniform consisting of a navy blue jumper, long-sleeved white blouse, white bobby socks, and black and white saddle shoes. It was easy for me to get ready quickly, since I never had to take time choosing what clothes to put on each morning. On one occasion, I got a bad sunburn at the beach. My back, arms, and legs were bright red, and I experienced such agony that I had to be excused from wearing the uniform. Some of my classmates were jealous because I got permission to wear loose fitting, casual clothing, but I wished I could have worn my uniform rather than being in such pain.

Daughters of Wisdom, the order of nuns at the school, originated in France more than three hundred years ago. They were an inspiration to me. Here's the school's alma mater that I still remember singing with the other students:

Daughters of Wisdom over the sea
God sent you yearning and burning for me.
Life's tender loveliness fondly ye teach
Heavenly heights ye prompt us to reach.
Daughters of Wisdom gladly and free
Thy memories will follow o'er life's troubled seas.
Doors of Wisdom open wide, loyal daughters gather near
Years of happiness inside, years of hope and love and cheer.
Halls of Wisdom ever we'll be
True to God and self and thee.

One of the memories I have of this school was a special day set aside for our senior class. A dynamic priest led the full-day session, which focused on learning more about God and our relationship with Him. Although I can no longer recall the details of his presentation, I felt encouraged by what he shared and the time flew by quickly.

As a teen, I liked babysitting to make extra money. I babysat regularly for one neighbor's two children, but I wasn't always available.

Whenever she found out I couldn't make it, she'd ask if my brother Al would babysit. What a relief for her when he could fill in for me. I also babysat a number of times for a Jewish boy about four and a half years old. One evening after his parents left to go out, he said to me, "You're a Gentile."

I didn't respond because I had no idea what he was talking about. Sometime later, I found out that a Gentile is a person who is not a Jew. Obviously I qualified.

Al and Jim were slim as teenagers so they wanted to put on extra pounds. Even though they ate a lot, it was difficult for them to gain weight. After taking a dietary supplement called "Weight On" for awhile, they were happy to start gaining weight. Here I was trying to lose weight and they were desperate to gain some.

I have great memories of our family backyard barbecues. One of my favorite treats was "bacon bread." We bought freshly baked potato bread from the local bakery and cut it into thick, one-inch slices. We used a large, rectangular chunk of fatty bacon about two inches thick, with the skin left on it to hold the bacon together while grilling. One of my parents held the bacon over the charcoal grill with a long-handled fork. While it cooked, my parents took the bacon and moved it over to a plate with thick slices of bread to absorb the bacon fat drippings. This process continued until the bread was well-soaked with the drippings. Then we added pepper and thinly sliced, raw onions and ate the delicious bacon bread. The barbecues also included hamburgers, pork sausages, or chicken.

When it came to breakfast, I loved bacon and eggs with buttered toast. After frying the bacon and removing it from the pan, Mom cooked the eggs in the remaining bacon fat, which added extra flavor to the eggs. My mouth waters whenever I think about the delicious taste of this breakfast. Those were the days when we didn't know about high cholesterol and its detrimental effects. If something tasted good, we ate and enjoyed it without giving it a second thought.

As a family, we frequently looked forward to ice cream for dessert. It was exciting to see a Carvel ice cream stand being built on a side street across from our corner house, and we couldn't wait until it opened. Carvel served soft ice cream rather than the scoops of hard ice cream that we were accustomed to. It tasted richer and creamier than regular ice cream, and at the time they didn't have a low-fat version. When relatives and friends came to visit, they often bought my brothers and me ice cream cones. What a delicious treat!

During my last year in high school, I began to think seriously about attending college. However, I wasn't sure what course of study to pursue. We had a close Hungarian friend of the family, Imre, who worked as a pharmacist for a pharmaceutical company. After having a few conversations with him, I thought about going into the same field. I requested course information from Saint John's University in Jamaica, New York. I reviewed the curriculum and decided to apply to the College of Pharmacy. How excited I felt to receive a letter of acceptance.

My cousin Alex volunteered to teach me to drive when I turned eighteen, which was the minimum age required for driving in New York City. He and his mother, my Aunt Helen, lived in Middle Village, about eight minutes away from our home by car. They have always been very dear to me. We got together frequently because they lived nearer than our other relatives. I appreciated the many hours Alex took me out in his car to practice driving in preparation for the road test. After I got the license, my parents purchased a car. I was thrilled to be the first in my family to have a driver's license.

I commuted to the university by car, which took about thirty-five minutes. It was much more convenient than when I had used public transportation to get to school. Shortly after starting my classes, I found out how much more in-depth and difficult they were compared to high school. I spent at least six hours a day completing assignments and studying for tests at home and in the university library. With my leisure time limited during the school year, I looked forward to the summer when I had a job and more free time.

My parents were always supportive when I went through challenging times with my college courses. Their love and positive words of encouragement helped me to persevere and stay focused during times when I felt like giving up.

I liked getting to know many of my classmates. One in particular who became a dear friend was Carol from Connecticut, who was also pursuing a degree in pharmacy. She rented a room from an elderly couple in a house near the campus. On some weekends, she came over on either Saturday or Sunday for the day. Carol and I studied and enjoyed spending time together away from school. She looked forward to Mom's delicious cooking and baking. We treated her like part of the family, and to this day, we keep in touch and get together from time to time.

One of the interesting subjects I took was pharmacology, which is the science of drugs, including their composition, uses, and effects. This course also had a laboratory class, where students were assigned to work together in groups of three. We had to test certain drugs on mice and determine what effect the drugs had on them. I was fortunate to work with others in my group who didn't mind handling the mice, because I wanted nothing to do with touching the little critters.

After graduation, I started a six-month internship at a Catholic hospital in midtown Manhattan, which turned into a permanent position. The head pharmacist and supervisor of the pharmacy was Sister Donata, a nun about sixty years old. I couldn't have asked to work for a nicer person. Her kindness, cheerful attitude, and pleasant smile brightened up the work atmosphere. She lived across the street from the hospital.

To get to the hospital, I had to walk fifteen minutes from home to the subway station and wait a few minutes for the train. The ride into the city took at least thirty minutes, and then I walked five minutes to the hospital.

I worked daytime hours during the week except for Thursdays when I stayed until nine o'clock in the evening. Including my supervisor, there were seven pharmacists. We took turns working different nights. Our responsibilities included dispensing prescriptions at both the hospital pharmacy and the out-patient clinic located in a building adjacent to the hospital. In addition, we used pharmaceutical-grade ingredients to make large quantities of lotions, ointments, and creams. My co-workers were friendly and I enjoyed my job.

On the way to work one day, I waited for the train on the subway station platform. I decided to buy a box of peppermint-flavored Chiclets gum from a vending machine. Each small box contained two square pieces of candy-coated gum. I put a penny into the slot, turned the knob, and got the gum I paid for. To my surprise and delight, boxes of gum kept coming out of the machine nonstop. It seemed as if I had hit the jackpot. I filled my jacket pockets until the train arrived.

In thinking back to my growing up years, I'm thankful that I grew up in a family where I felt loved and cherished. Mom and Dad and the nuns at the various schools I attended were role models who had a positive influence on my life. I'm also thankful for my two wonderful younger brothers, who have always meant a lot to me.

Chapter 4

Late Night Encounter

Y LIFE FOREVER changed on a Saturday night in mid-September 1968. I was twenty-five years old and lived at home with my parents in Rego Park, New York. My brothers were away at college.

I expected it to be nothing more than a night out at the movies with my friends, Kathy and Steffie, sisters two years apart in age. They lived in Kew Gardens, fifteen minutes away from my home by car. I drove to their place, picked them up, and we went to a local movie theater on Continental Avenue in Forest Hills.

After leaving the theater, I said, "That was a good movie."

Kathy, the older sister, said, "Yolanda, let's go to Pep McGuire's and try to meet some guys! It's a pub in Kew Gardens, five minutes from where we live."

"Have you been there before?" I asked.

"Yes, we like the place," Kathy replied.

"They have a band, dance floor, and bar," Steffie said.

"Okay." I was tired and ready to call it a night but I agreed, not wanting to be a party pooper.

At 11:00 P.M. we arrived at Pep McGuire's, located along Queens Boulevard, a major highway through Queens leading to Manhattan. The pub stood between a row of other business establishments that lined the city block. Just inside the entrance, I saw a postage-stamp-size dance floor to the left, with a three-piece band playing. On the right side of the room was an oval-shaped bar surrounded by about a dozen people.

I anticipated seeing many more people there on a Saturday night. I thought, *I don't think I'll be meeting anyone here tonight.*

"Kathy, is this place usually so empty on Saturday nights?"

"No. The other times when Steffie and I were here, there were a lot more people."

The band caught my attention because it played lively music I liked. There were only two couples dancing. As the three of us girls stood by the bar holding drinks and talking, I felt a gentle tap on my right shoulder. When I turned around, a nice-looking guy, about six feet tall with neatly combed, dark brown hair and a charming smile, asked, "Would you like to dance?"

"Yes." I smiled back. I put my drink down on the bar.

He took my hand gently and walked me to the dance floor. We introduced ourselves and that's when I met Tom. His warmth came through in his smile and tender touch while we danced. I thought, *What a nice guy. I'm glad he asked me to dance.*

He surprised me when he said, "Yolanda is a pretty name."

"Thank you." He certainly scored points with me after that compliment. I liked him from the start because he made me feel at ease when we chatted, as if we had known each other for a long time.

While slow dancing, I asked Tom, "What kind of work do you do?"

"Right now, I'm a full-time student at New York University in the Bronx, and I'm studying mechanical engineering. I'll be graduating next year, in June 1969."

"Did you go to the university right after high school?"

"No. I went to New York City Community College in Brooklyn after graduating from Forest Hills High School. I got a two-year associate's degree in mechanical technology. At the time, I didn't plan to continue my schooling."

"What were your plans?"

Tom paused, looked at me seriously, and replied, "All I wanted to do was get a job. After working for three different companies over a two-year period, I felt dissatisfied with my career. That's when I decided to pursue a bachelor's degree in engineering, which meant another four years of college."

"Was it challenging going back to school?"

"Yes, especially in the beginning. I found some of the courses extremely difficult, and at times I wasn't sure I'd make it through them."

I looked at Tom compassionately. "I know what you mean, because I found many of my courses to be difficult, and there were times I wondered if I'd ever get a pharmacy degree."

"What college did you attend, Yolanda?"

"St. John's University."

"What are you doing now?"

"I work as a hospital pharmacist in Manhattan and I love my job."

As we continued talking, Tom enthusiastically mentioned, "I recently read an interesting book called *Think and Grow Rich* by Napoleon Hill."

My eyes opened wide and my jaw dropped. I stared at him in disbelief. "Wow! I can't believe it! I just finished reading that book too."

"Are you serious, Yolanda?"

"Yes!"

"That's amazing," Tom said.

"It is!" I exclaimed.

We looked at each other with a big smile, our eyes lighting up with excitement. Our common interest in the book strengthened the bond that was forming between us.

We stopped dancing and went over to my girlfriends at the bar. I introduced them to Tom. After talking with them a few minutes, we went back to dancing and a lengthy discussion about the book.

Some time after 1:00 A.M., the band started packing up to leave. Tom and I were the only ones left on the dance floor. We walked a few steps to the bar and continued talking nonstop.

Tom said, "I came here tonight much later than at any time in the past because relatives were visiting my mom and me. They stayed longer than usual."

"Really?"

"Yeah, I normally don't go out so late, but tonight was different. I had a strong feeling about coming to Pep McGuire's tonight, regardless of the late hour."

It turned out he had arrived a short time before my friends and I got there. *What perfect timing,* I told myself. *Meeting each other seems like much more than just a chance encounter.*

I felt exhilarated being with Tom and I didn't want the evening to end anytime soon. We enjoyed each other's company so much that the hours flew by quickly. We completely lost track of time until the place closed. When I left with my girlfriends, Tom and I walked in front of them to my car parked three blocks away. When we got there, Tom looked at me tenderly and asked, "Can I have your phone number, Yolanda?"

I smiled broadly and replied, "Yes. When will you call me?"

I surprised myself with my question. *This is the first time I ever asked a guy I just met when he planned to call me.*

He hesitated a few moments and said, "I'll call you Monday night."

"I'm looking forward to hearing from you."

I dropped off Kathy and Steffie. On the way home, all I could think about was Tom. *What a fantastic time we had. I can't wait to get his call and go out on a date.*

Chapter 5

Cloud Nine

AFTER GETTING OUT of college, I had dated several guys over a two-year period, but not seriously. One day my dad had said, "Yolanda, I don't understand why you haven't met someone yet that you really like. I stop at church sometimes on the way to work and pray for you to meet the right man."

"Thanks for your prayers, Dad. When I find the right guy I'll know it."

By the time I reached age twenty-five, I guess he figured it was time for me to settle down and get married.

The Sunday morning after meeting Tom at the pub, I couldn't wait to tell Mom about him and the great time we had getting acquainted. I said, "He told me that my name is pretty."

Her eyes lit up and she smiled. "Yolanda is a beautiful name."

"No other guy ever said that to me before. And you won't believe it, Mom, we just finished reading the same book, *Think and Grow Rich*."

"Really?"

"Yes. We never stopped talking, and I enjoyed being with him."

"I can tell you never felt as interested in anyone else."

"You're right. He plans to call me Monday night. I can't wait to hear from him!"

Monday at work seemed to drag, since I couldn't wait to get home and receive Tom's call that evening. After supper, I could barely sit still on the couch, waiting for the phone to ring. I had butterflies in my stomach. When the phone rang, I jumped up and rushed to get it. Just hearing Tom's voice energized me and made my day. We spoke a few minutes and then he asked, "Are you available this Friday night to see a movie?"

"Yes, that sounds great."

"Can I pick you up at 7 o'clock?"

"Yes." I gave Tom my address.

"Yolanda, I'm looking forward to seeing you again."

"I feel the same way, Tom. See you Friday." We said goodbye. What a delight to anticipate seeing him in four days.

Throughout the week, I reflected back to our phone conversation and the previous Saturday night. Wonderful thoughts ran through my head. *What perfect timing the way we met at the pub. He's such a gentleman. We had so much to talk about. I can't wait to see him again.*

When Friday night arrived and the doorbell rang, I opened the door and felt elated to see Tom standing there.

"Hi, Yolanda."

"Hi, Tom. Come in. Let me introduce you to my mom."

"Hello, Mrs. Gyuricza. It's a pleasure to meet you," he said with a smile.

"Nice to meet you too, Tom." Mom smiled.

We talked with her a few minutes before leaving to go on our date. They hit it off well, and Mom seemed to like him right away.

After a ten-minute drive, Tom parked his car, and we walked a couple of blocks to the theater. I can't remember what movie played that night. However, I do recall that about half an hour after it started, Tom reached over and held my hand gently. I thought, *It feels so natural holding hands, as if I've known him a long time.*

When the movie ended, we walked to a nearby restaurant and ordered hamburgers, fries, and soda. As we sat across from each other at the table, we chatted enthusiastically and found ourselves without a loss for words as the hours flew by. When Tom took me home, we kissed goodnight at the front door and expressed how much we enjoyed our evening together. He said, "I'll call you during the week to set up a date for next Friday or Saturday night."

"That sounds terrific! I'm looking forward to seeing you again."

We continued going out on weekends, which progressed into seeing each other during the week on occasion. One day Tom said, "I want to see you more often, but my time is limited. I need to stay focused on all the homework, projects, and studying for tests. I can't wait to graduate."

"I can appreciate what you're going through because my last year of college was extremely busy too."

"Thanks for understanding, Yolanda."

My life centered around Tom and I knew he cared for me very much. Our relationship blossomed, and before we knew it, we were head over heels for each other. Little did we realize after meeting at the pub how dramatically our lives would change.

After five months of dating between September 1968 and February 1969, I believed Tom was definitely the man I wanted to marry. I sensed he felt the same way about me, but the topic of marriage never came up, and I didn't want to put him under any pressure.

Tom and I didn't go to church together on Sundays, since we attended different churches close to our homes, nor did we see each other that day of the week because of the time he needed to do school work. However, he happened to be free on Sunday, February 9th. He planned to drive over and pick me up to attend my church. I awoke at nine o'clock to get ready. I looked out the window, and it caught me by surprise to see that a large amount of snow had fallen overnight. Light snow continued to fall.

At the same time, the phone rang. It was Tom. He said, "I can't drive over to pick you up as we planned, because the snow is at least a foot deep and my street isn't plowed."

"Tom, I'm disappointed we won't be able to see each other today."

"I have an idea, Yolanda. We can walk to Continental Avenue and meet at the movie theater. Then we can continue on to the Catholic church that isn't far from there."

"That sounds like a good idea."

"Can you get ready and leave your home in an hour?"

"Yes."

"Yolanda, it will probably take each of us about forty-five minutes to walk to the theater from our homes in the deep snow. Is that okay with you?"

"Sure. I'm glad we can still get together."

"Me too. I'll see you soon."

After saying goodbye, I hurried to get ready so I could leave by ten o'clock.

We lived a few miles apart but only around one mile from where we agreed to meet. After leaving home, I found it challenging to walk in the deep snow. I got to the theater just after Tom arrived. What a relief to meet and proceed to the church where we finally got to warm up after being out in the cold. Afterwards, we hiked back to my house hand in hand, trudging through the snow. We arrived there early in the afternoon, tired and hungry.

When we got inside the front door, Mom smiled and said, "Hi, I'm glad to see you. I have stuffed peppers cooking on the stove."

"Mom, you're making one of my favorite meals."

"I know. That's why I made it."

Tom and I walked over to the large pot of peppers and I removed the lid. We looked at the green peppers simmering in tomato sauce. I told Tom, "The peppers are filled with a mixture of ground beef, grated onions, eggs, and rice. Don't they look delicious?"

"Yes, I can't wait to eat."

"Tom, I love the aroma."

"It smells wonderful, Yolanda."

"It'll be ready in thirty minutes," Mom said. "You and Tom must be tired and hungry after all the walking in the snow."

"We are. When Dad gets home from work after midnight, he'll be happy you made stuffed peppers."

"Yes, he will."

Tom and I sat in the living room and talked while waiting to eat. When the food was ready, Mom yelled from the kitchen, "Come and get it!"

Tom and I couldn't wait to start eating after seeing the stuffed peppers with tomato sauce steaming in our bowls. When Mom came to the table, we began to enjoy the scrumptious meal.

After his first spoonful, Tom raved, "This is fantastic, Mrs. Gyuricza." He quickly shoveled down more.

Mom smiled. "I'm glad you're enjoying it, Tom."

He nodded with his mouth full and eyes wide open.

We finished eating, and Tom and I thanked Mom for the delicious meal. I helped her clean up while Tom relaxed in the living room. After she and I were done, we joined him. As the three of us chatted, the time passed quickly and it started to get dark.

Tom began to get ready to leave. I could tell he didn't feel much like walking two miles in the snow at night to get home. I felt bad for him. I asked Mom, "Can Tom stay overnight since it's getting late and the walk back home will take him a long time?"

"Yes, he's welcome to stay. He can sleep in the spare bedroom downstairs."

Tom was relieved and said, "Thank you, Mrs. Gyuricza." He called his mom to let her know his plans to spend the night at my house due to the storm.

Earlier that day, Tom and I had worn leather boots that got heavily soaked after walking in the snow. We had taken them off after arriving at my place. I had changed into shoes, but he was still walking around in socks.

When I went to show Tom the spare bedroom, I stood behind him at the top of the stairs to let him walk down ahead of me. He took his first step on the uncarpeted, wooden stairs and suddenly he slipped. I watched in horror as he bounced down each step on his backside with a loud thud, from the top of the stairway all the way to the bottom. It happened so quickly, and there he was sitting on the floor. As I ran down to help him I cried out, "Are you okay?"

"I think I am, except for pain in my legs and back."

"Can you get up?"

"Let me try."

"I'll help you." What a relief to see him stand and walk around.

Mom came to the stairway to see what happened. I told her and she said, "Thank God he's okay."

Tom and I stayed downstairs and talked awhile. Out of the blue, he took my hands, held them in his, and looked at me affectionately. He

31

kept looking into my eyes and then leaned forward to kiss me. After the kiss, he took me by surprise when he said, "Yolanda, I love you very much. Will you marry me?"

"Yes!" I responded without hesitation. "I love you very much too."

We kissed again, and when our lips touched, it felt like fireworks were going off all around me. My level of excitement went through the roof after hearing Tom's proposal. We wrapped our arms around each other and enjoyed this special moment.

I wanted to tell Mom right away. We went upstairs as quickly as we could with Tom still recovering from his fall. I exclaimed, "Mom, Tom just asked me to marry him!"

"Congratulations!" She looked very happy to hear the exciting news. Then she laughed and said, "Tom fell twice in one day, first down the stairs and again for my daughter."

Chapter 6

Balloons Bursting

ONE DAY EARLY in November 1968, I got home from work and greeted my mom with a kiss on the cheek as I normally did. She usually had a smile on her face and looked happy to see me, but that day was different. I couldn't help but notice the fearful expression on her face. I thought, *Mom's eyes are red and it looks like she's been crying.*

"What's the matter, Mom? Is something wrong?"

"Within the last few weeks, I started to feel painful lumps in my breasts. I'm afraid it might be cancer."

"Oh, Mom, I hope not. You need to be examined right away. Tomorrow, after I get to work at the hospital, I'll try to talk with a doctor I know who is a gynecologist. His name is Dr. Green. He has a good reputation. Hopefully I can set up an appointment for you to see him as soon as possible."

My brothers were away at college and Dad was at work. Mom and I had dinner. Neither of us talked while we ate. I can't remember anything more about the evening except that I went to bed much earlier than usual because I felt emotionally drained after what Mom had shared with me.

The next day after I got to work, I spoke with Dr. Green and he agreed to examine my mother. He told me to call his office and make an appointment, which I did immediately. Fortunately, he could see her the following week.

The day of Mom's examination, I took off from work to go with her. We went by subway to the office in Manhattan, located about three blocks from the hospital where I worked. We hardly talked on the way there. *I'm sure Mom is dreading the checkup,* I thought.

I said, "Mom, I know you're worried about the exam."

"Yes, I am, Yolanda."

I tried to reassure her. "He's an excellent doctor and he should be able to help you."

"I hope so. I'm trying to leave everything in God's hands."

After Mom saw Dr. Green, he scheduled her for a biopsy to evaluate the breast tissue. A few days later, Mom went for the biopsy. The following week, she was scheduled for another appointment with him to find out the results. Waiting for the outcome made me feel anxious and afraid. I thought, *I can't even imagine how Mom is feeling.*

During the time between the first and second appointments, Mom and I tried to remain optimistic and we hoped for the best. I'm not sure how my dad was handling things because he and I didn't talk about what Mom was going through.

Mom and I went together to the doctor's office for her follow-up visit. We sat in the waiting room for fifteen minutes before a nurse brought us to a private room. Dr. Green came into the room with a look of concern and compassion and said, "Mrs. Gyuricza, I'm very sorry. The prognosis is malignant cancer. You need to have a radical mastectomy for both breasts."

Mom's face turned pale, and with a trembling voice, she asked, "How long can I wait before having the operation?"

"You should have it done as soon as possible. I'd like to schedule it during the second week in December."

"That's only two weeks away," Mom said.

"Is that okay with you, Mrs. Gyuricza?"

"Yes."

Fear gripped me as I sat with Mom listening to Dr. Green. I felt sick to my stomach, and my body was numb. Tears welled up in Mom's eyes and mine. We didn't talk much after leaving the doctor's office. On the way home, I said, "Mom, I'll be praying the operation will be successful and that everything goes well."

"Thanks, Yolanda. I appreciate your prayers."

The next few weeks leading up to the operation seemed to drag by. During that time, Mom and I tried to act as if everything were normal. When I came home from work, we spent quiet evenings together while Dad was at work. I tried to remain positive around Mom, but I was struggling deep down inside because of my concern for her.

What a big relief when the operation was over and Mom left the hospital the following week. It was wonderful having Mom home again and seeing her recuperate. I helped her as much as possible with household chores and cooking meals.

Within the next two months, Mom seemed to be in good spirits and on her way to a full recovery. She went through a series of radiation treatments after the surgery. As far as I could tell, Mom appeared to be getting back to normal after the operation, both physically and emotionally.

In early March, Mom and Dad wanted to start planning for the wedding. Along with my parents, Tom and I found a reception hall and set the wedding date for August 16th, 1969. That was the easy part of the planning process. Selecting the band created the first conflict that led to a downward spiral from that point on.

Mom insisted that a particular Hungarian band should play at the wedding reception. She said to Tom and me, "They're a great band, and they can play the Hungarian songs Dad and I like."

I wondered if they could play the popular songs that Tom and I liked.

The tone of her voice was insistent. She obviously felt strongly about hiring the band, which may have been partially because her brother, Bela, would be coming to the wedding from Hungary. She had not seen him for thirty-five years.

I looked at Tom and he nodded "yes" and I turned to Mom and said, "We'll set up an appointment to hear the band play."

"I'm sure you'll be pleased," Mom said.

After Tom and I went to see them, I said to Mom, "We listened to the band but were frustrated because they weren't familiar with any of the popular American songs that we asked them to play."

"I'm sorry you didn't care for them," she said in a harsh tone of voice.

I gently responded, "Tom and I want to check out the reception hall's house band."

Mom didn't say a word, but her disapproval came through loud and clear. She glared at me and placed her hands on her hips. Her body was rigid and tense. Her lips were pursed in anger. I didn't know what to say, so I kept silent.

The house band turned out to be fantastic. They could play all the songs we requested. After I told Mom how much Tom and I liked the house band, she said abruptly, "If you don't use the Hungarian band, you'll have to pay for the other band!"

"Mom, we'll be glad to pay for the band."

With tears in her eyes, she said, "I'm disappointed you don't want the Hungarian band to play at your wedding."

"I understand. I'm sorry it didn't work out the way you had hoped."

It appeared to me the band issue was settled, in spite of the fact that I perceived Mom had hard feelings because Tom and I didn't care for the band she wanted.

In mid-April, Mom and I went to a local bridal shop. The owner and seamstress showed us sample wedding gowns she had made. After I started looking at them with Mom, I said, "They're all lovely. It will be hard to choose one."

"Yes, you're right," Mom said.

As we continued to look, I saw one that jumped out at me and I shouted, "This is the one I like best. It's beautiful. I love it!"

Mom agreed. "It is beautiful. This one will be perfect for you."

In talking with the seamstress, we learned some interesting details about the gown. It was made of white tulle, which is a thin, fine netting named after a city named Tulle, in France, where the fabric originated. The gown was lined with white taffeta, a crisp and lightweight nylon fabric. White lace flowers covered the front and back of the gown above the waist, as well as the unlined sleeves. Miniature white pearls, one-sixteenth inch in diameter, surrounded the center of each flower, and shiny sequins were enclosed within the pearls. Scattered lace flowers covered the rest of the gown, and the bottom eight inches around the gown hem had scalloped lace.

The train attached to the back of the gown measured two yards in length and was made of a double layer of tulle. The lace pattern on the train matched the gown, but didn't include the pearls and sequins.

My headdress, the tiara, consisted of thirty white plastic flowers with a rhinestone in the center of each flower. The leaves of the flowers were made with white lace and decorated with miniature pearls bordering each leaf. At the tip of each leaf, just inside the pearl border, was a single rhinestone. The comb portion of the tiara had two veils attached to it. The top veil measured twenty-two inches long, and the bottom one was three yards in length with lace along the edges.

Before we left the bridal shop, the owner said, "I'm glad you found something you like. Let me take your measurements. I'll call you when the gown is ready, and we'll set up an appointment for you to come back."

"I'm looking forward to returning and trying it on." I thought, *I love the gorgeous gown and can't wait to wear it on my wedding day.*

When we left, Mom said, "I'll pay for the wedding gown."

"Thank you."

Within a few weeks after going to the bridal shop with Mom, I had a feeling something was bothering her. She seemed irritable and tense.

I asked, "Is everything okay, Mom?"

"Yes."

"Is there anything you want to talk about?"

"No."

Despite Mom's response, I knew something was wrong, but we weren't talking the way we used to. I felt a strain in our relationship, which had begun when Tom and I hadn't agreed to use the Hungarian band for the wedding. I thought, *Maybe if my parents could get away to rest and relax, there would be less tension between Mom and me.*

I had an idea but didn't feel comfortable bringing it up to Mom. I approached Dad and said, "It might be a good idea for you to take Mom on a trip to Florida for a week. I'll pay all your expenses."

"That sounds great, Yolanda. I'd love to go, but I'm not sure how Mom will feel about it. I'll talk with her and let you know."

A few days later, Dad came to me and said, "I talked with Mom and told her I thought it would be good for us to take the trip and that you wanted to pay for it. She told me she wasn't interested in going away at this time."

"I'm sorry she feels that way, Dad." *It seemed like such a good idea.*

"Me too."

Even though I wasn't happy to find out Mom's response, I tried not to let it get to me.

Early in June, Tom graduated from New York University and started working for an engineering firm in Manhattan. Now that we both had jobs in New York City, we planned to live in Queens after getting married.

My family home had a downstairs apartment with a kitchen, living room, bathroom, and bedroom. Before my brothers left for college, they shared the bedroom. The apartment was accessible with a stairway from the first floor of our home, and it had a private front and back door entrance at ground level.

After I got home from work one day, Mom came into my bedroom and in a demanding tone of voice, she said, "You and Tom will have to live in our downstairs apartment after you get married. I need your help taking care of the house since I don't have the strength I had before the operation."

Mom's insistence took me by surprise. I was caught totally off guard. *What can I say to Mom? She's being unreasonable.*

I had to catch my breath. With my heart pounding furiously and a huge knot in the pit of my stomach, I said with a shaky voice, "Mom, I'll talk about it with Tom and get back to you." *I don't think he's going to like her idea. I know I won't be able to deal with it.*

I suddenly realized why she had asked Dad to take a week off from work to paint and wallpaper downstairs. It was to prepare our "future apartment."

When I told Tom about Mom's plans, he said, "I don't feel good about living in the downstairs apartment."

"Neither do I. We need to be on our own when we get married, Tom."

"Definitely."

I dreaded telling Mom our decision. I knew she wouldn't be happy. She was sitting in the living room. I went to her and said, "Tom and I discussed what you had in mind for our living arrangements after we get married. Closer to the wedding, we'll be looking for an apartment that won't be too far from here. I'll still be able to help you out."

Mom's face turned red, and tears trickled down her cheeks. She stood up, abruptly turned away from me, and walked out of the room.

One Friday night, Tom picked me up for a date. I got in the car and he said, "Today my boss asked me to consider taking a job assignment in Vermont. I'd be working at a nuclear power plant construction site. It could possibly work out for us to go there right after we get married. It might be a great opportunity. What do you think?"

"It sounds good, Tom."

"Of course, you'd have to quit your job. Is that okay with you?"

"Yes, I'll go anywhere with you, but I don't think it's the right time to tell my mom. She's still upset because we don't want to live downstairs. Let's wait before telling her anything about your job transfer until it's finalized."

"That's a good idea, Yolanda."

During the last week in June, the bridal shop owner called and told me the wedding gown was ready. After I got off the phone, I said to Mom, "My gown is ready! I can't wait to try it on! Do you want to go with me?"

"No. I don't feel up to it."

I went to the bridal shop. I loved how the gown looked on me. *I wish Mom had come along to share this exciting moment.*

I paid for the gown and was thrilled to take it with me. I went home and felt uneasy about reminding Mom that she had wanted to buy it for me. She never mentioned anything, so I decided not to bring it up.

In the beginning of July, Tom found out his transfer to Vermont was finalized. We planned to move there after our wedding in August. Neither of us owned a car. A new Chevy Impala caught our attention at a local car dealership. After driving it, we felt it was the right vehicle for us. With Tom just starting a job out of college, he had no money saved yet. I had worked three years after attending college and had saved enough to pay cash for the car.

When I told Mom our plans to move away from New York because of Tom's job assignment in Vermont, she started crying and yelled, "How can you leave me and go to Vermont when I need you here?"

Chapter 7

Drug Overdose

THROUGH THE MONTH of July, I felt tension mounting between Mom and me. I started getting headaches almost daily and had trouble sleeping at night. I'd wake up in the morning feeling exhausted. As much as I loved my mother and wanted peace between us, it was increasingly difficult to get along. I was distraught over the breakdown in communication. *Mom and I have always had a close relationship. I wish this weren't happening.*

I was thankful that at least things were going well with my job as a hospital pharmacist. My supervisor, a Catholic nun, had always been pleasant and kind, and my work environment provided a welcome diversion from what was going on at home. However, when I got to work one morning, Sister Donata called me into her office unexpectedly and asked me to sit down. She said, "Your mother phoned and told me about conflicts going on between the two of you."

My body started feeling numb and my stomach felt queasy. *Why would Mom call her? These problems are between Mom and me.*

It took me a few moments to gain my composure. After quietly taking several deep breaths, I responded, "I can't believe she called you. There's no reason you should be involved in personal issues between my mother and me."

"You're right, Yolanda, but she certainly sounded convincing about your being at fault. She said you're not acting normal and that you need psychiatric care."

I sat there in total shock and disbelief. My head was pounding. My hands were trembling. *Am I going to lose my job?*

I didn't want to say too much, so I briefly shared what was going on from my perspective. *Does Sister Donata believe anything I'm telling her from my point of view?* I got the impression she may have sided with my mother. After all, it would be very unusual for a supervisor to receive a phone call from an employee's mother and hear things that should have remained private.

I left her office. My mind was racing. *How am I supposed to concentrate on work?* I asked myself. *I just want to leave the hospital and take off the rest of the day.*

I had to force myself to stay at work and act as if everything was okay. Consequently, I not only felt under pressure at home, but after Mom's phone call, I started feeling stressed at work.

After my anger had been simmering all day long, I arrived home from work knowing I had to confront Mom. When I walked in the door and saw her standing in the kitchen, I wanted to scream at her for what she had done. However, I managed to control myself.

In a sharp tone of voice, I said, "I can't believe you talked with Sister Donata. She called me into her office and told me what you said about me. I felt horrified and embarrassed."

With hardly any emotion, Mom looked at me and said, "What I said to her is true, Yolanda."

After hearing Mom's response, I turned around and walked away. I realized there was nothing more I could say because it was obvious it wouldn't change the way she felt. I called Tom from the phone extension in my room and told him about my day.

He said, "I'm sorry to hear what happened. You won't be working at the hospital much longer. Next month we'll be married and living in Vermont. Just try to hang in there for now."

"I can't wait to get married, Tom."

"Me too, Yolanda."

After Mom's phone call, I started feeling uneasy at the hospital. I sensed Sister Donata may have been wondering if I was still capable of doing my job as a pharmacist. I tried my best not to become sidetracked emotionally because I had to think clearly and stay focused at work.

Normally, during my half hour lunch break, I relaxed in the hospital cafeteria while eating a sandwich. However, due to my soaring stress level, I changed my lunchtime routine and went to a locker room across from the pharmacy to gulp down my sandwich. Then I rushed to a church around the corner from the hospital to attend Mass and receive communion. The time in church gave me some degree of comfort.

During my fifteen-minute morning breaks, I often called Tom at his workplace to confide in him. He was the only one I could talk with about the distress I was experiencing at home and at work.

Going home after work became more and more difficult. Mom and I hardly spoke with each other. Talking with her usually turned into a confrontation. I tried to stay out of her way.

I had been having difficulty sleeping through the night for at least two weeks. As my anxiety level skyrocketed, it got to the point where I tossed and turned all night and got no sleep.

Mom was taking prescription sleeping pills, as needed, after her operation. I was desperate to get some sleep. It seemed like sleeping pills were the only solution. I found the bottle of pills in the bathroom cabinet with only a few left. Without Mom's knowledge, I decided to refill the prescription and use it for myself. To my dismay, taking the prescribed dosage before bedtime helped me to get only three or four hours of sleep a night.

Each morning when I crawled out of bed, I felt like I hadn't slept at all. *How am I going to get through the day?* I thought. *I'm so tired. I can't get enough sleep. I feel stressed out living at home.*

Due to the enormous mental and emotional anguish that plagued me, I knew I had to find another place to live. The only one I could turn to was Tom. I called him from the hospital and said, "I need to leave home and find a place to live until we get married. You know what I'm going through."

"Yes, I do. I'll talk with my mom and ask her if it's okay for you to stay with us."

"Thanks, Tom."

He called his mom right away from work and explained my situation. I was relieved when Tom called me back and said, "My mother told me you can come and live at our place."

Rescued

"I'm relieved. I'll have to thank your mother."

"I'll see you tonight, Yolanda."

"I can't wait, Tom."

That evening, I went home and packed a suitcase in my bedroom with the door closed while Mom was in the kitchen. When Tom arrived, we went down the hallway to my bedroom and got the suitcase. Before we left, I walked up to Mom and said, "I'll be leaving home and staying with Tom and his mother until we get married."

As we went to the front door to leave, Mom said in a loud, angry tone of voice, "I can't believe what you're doing!"

Neither Tom nor I said a word. We walked out the front door to the car.

Tom knew I was taking sleeping pills. After moving in with him and his mom, I continued taking them. However, even in the peaceful atmosphere of Tom's home, I continued to have trouble getting enough sleep.

On the first Friday night after I arrived there, Tom's brother Vin came over for dinner. After the meal, I said, "Everything was delicious, Mrs. Barbagallo. Thank you."

"You're welcome, Yolanda."

"Please excuse me. I'm very tired and need to go upstairs to bed." *I'm desperate for sleep. My body is ready to collapse.*

Shortly after I awoke the next morning, Tom knocked on the bedroom door. While I was still lying in bed, he came in and sat on the edge of the bed. He gently took my hands in his, looked at me affectionately, and asked, "Yolanda, do you remember anything other than falling asleep last night?"

"No. What do you mean?"

Tom explained, "About an hour after you went to bed, I came upstairs to check on you and see whether you were able to fall asleep. At first it appeared you were in a very deep sleep. As I leaned over and got close to your face to gently kiss you on the cheek, I realized you were hardly breathing. I frantically shook your shoulders, trying to wake you, and got no response. I yelled downstairs, 'There's something wrong with Yolanda! She's hardly breathing! We have to get her to the hospital immediately!'"

I was stunned. *This doesn't make any sense. I just came upstairs and went to bed last night.*

"What are you talking about?"

"This is what happened last night, Yolanda. It was terrifying. With you unconscious and your body limp as a rag doll, I carried you downstairs and out the door to Vin's car and laid you across the back seat. With Vin driving and me beside him, I sat, half-turned, in my seat with my left hand on your shoulder, silently begging God to spare your life."

Chills went through my entire body. *How could I have done this to myself, and to Tom?*

"I can't believe what you're telling me." *My mind is a total blank.* "I don't remember anything."

"We rushed you to the emergency room at Saint John's Hospital. The doctor decided to have your stomach pumped, based on my description of your drinking wine with supper and taking sleeping pills before going to bed. After you regained consciousness, you seemed to be totally unaware of what happened. The doctor kept you in the hospital an hour for observation before he released you. Vin drove us home and I put you to bed."

My thoughts were a blur as I desperately attempted to recall any details of the night before. "This is absolutely crazy. It blows me away. I just remember going to bed after supper and waking up this morning." *It's a miracle I'm here with Tom. I'm so thankful for him.*

With tears in his eyes, Tom said in a soft voice, "I panicked when I found you unconscious and couldn't wake you. My hands were shaking and my heart was pounding in my throat. All I could think of was rushing you to the hospital. I was afraid you might die. I'm grateful that Vin was over last night to help me get you to the hospital. He drove there as fast as he could. I felt like I was in a racecar."

"Thanks for taking care of me when I couldn't help myself." *Tom cares for me more than I could ever have imagined.*

"I'm thankful that you're alive, Yolanda."

"I appreciate what you and Vin did for me. I'm glad to be alive." *Without Tom, I probably wouldn't even be here after last night.*

"After you went upstairs, do you recall what you did before going to bed?"

"Yes. The last thing I remember is taking my usual sleeping pills and a few extra ones from sample packets I got at work. The samples were a different kind than the ones I normally took. I only tried the new pills because I had difficulty sleeping with the usual pills. I thought my body might have built up a tolerance to those, so trying the new pills seemed logical. I wasn't thinking straight, since I hadn't slept well for weeks leading up to last night. I guess the two glasses of wine I drank with supper probably increased the effect of the pills." *What was I thinking, taking the combination of pills and also drinking wine?*

Tom embraced me and held me tight for several moments and said, "I'm relieved you're okay and that I didn't lose you. I love you."

"I love you too, Tom." *How frightening to think that if Tom and Vin didn't get me to the hospital in time, I could have died.*

After this horrible experience, I prayed to God for the strength to get rid of the sleeping pills. I was determined to no longer take anything to help me sleep. I flushed the pills down the toilet.

I wondered, *Are things going to get better or worse before the wedding?*

Chapter 8

Nightmare

WHILE I STAYED at Tom's home, my mom called his mother at least once a day. Sometimes the calls were late at night. Having been awakened a number of times, she started taking the phone off the hook before going to bed. She had a job at a dress shop doing alterations and needed her rest.

One morning, Tom's mother approached me and said, "Yolanda, whenever your mom calls, she says you need psychiatric care."

"Mrs. Barbagallo, I can't understand why she keeps telling you I need professional help. I'm sorry you're getting disturbing phone calls from my mother."

My last day of work at the hospital was Friday, August 1st. That night after supper, Tom, his mother, Vin, and I were sitting in the living room talking. The front doorbell rang, and Tom went to see who it was. When he opened the door, he was surprised to see my mother standing there.

Tom said, "Hello, Mrs. Gyuricza, come in."

She walked in, and everyone stood up to greet her. In a loud and demanding tone of voice, she looked at Tom and Vin and said, "You have to take Yolanda to the hospital right away to have her admitted. She needs psychiatric help!"

"Mom, why are you doing this to me? I don't need to go to the hospital!"

"Yes, you do, Yolanda!"

"No, I don't!"

"Yes, you do!" she shouted.

I shouted back, "No, I don't, Mom! Will you please stop trying to get me admitted to the hospital?"

"Yolanda, you need to go there!"

I turned around and ran into the kitchen and down the stairway leading to the basement. Tom followed after me. I stood in the back of the basement and started sobbing. He walked up behind me, put his hand on my shoulder, and said, "I'm sorry this is happening to you. I don't agree with your mother."

With my back to him, I said with my voice quivering, "What do you think I should do? She's been trying to get me admitted to the hospital for the past month."

He said in a soft and calming voice, "Please look at me and listen to what I have to say."

I turned and looked at him with tears streaming down my face. He took my hands in his. "Yolanda, I know you don't need psychiatric care, but at this point it seems like the only way to convince your mother otherwise is to prove her wrong."

"Maybe you're right."

Tom kissed me gently and we embraced. I felt better after talking with him.

We walked back upstairs and into the living room. Tom's mother and brother appeared somewhat confused by the commotion. I still felt reluctant to give in to Mom.

Tom is probably right. The only way I can prove to Mom that I don't need professional help is to let Tom and Vin take me to the hospital. I said, "I don't want to argue about this anymore. I'll go."

Just before leaving, Mrs. Barbagallo said, "Yolanda, it won't work out for you to stay here any longer."

Tom's mother probably felt that if I weren't there, the phone calls would stop and she'd have peace and quiet once again.

Panic overcame me. *What am I going to do? I have no place to go. I feel sharp pains shooting through my lower back.*

Vin drove to Saint John's Hospital while Tom and I sat in the back seat. He put his arm around my shoulder and said, "Don't worry, I'm sure everything will work out."

"I hope you're right. I'm feeling overwhelmed because of the ongoing conflict between Mom and me."

"I don't believe you'll be admitted. Hopefully, after tonight your mom will stop trying to get you into the hospital for psychiatric care."

After arriving at the hospital, I was evaluated by a doctor. He determined I didn't need to be admitted. However, he scheduled me for an outpatient clinic appointment for the following Wednesday, which I planned to cancel.

I left the doctor's office and walked to where Tom and Vin were sitting in the waiting room. I said, "The doctor told me I'm free to leave."

Vin dropped us off where our car was parked near Tom's home. I had nowhere to sleep that night. Tom suggested I stay at a motel five minutes from his home. I agreed. When we got there, we found out the air conditioning wasn't working. We left and Tom drove west on Queens Boulevard, a ten-lane road. Between the towns of Elmhurst and Woodside, we found a motel along the boulevard. By now it was around 11 o'clock.

Tom booked a room and stayed with me for a few hours. We talked about the day's heart-wrenching events and our upcoming marriage. He said, "I'm looking forward to when we get married and move to Vermont. Then we can be free of the conflicts that have been going on."

"I know it's been hard for you, Tom, because of what I've been dealing with. I never expected we'd be going through so many challenges during our engagement. After what went on today at your house and my going to the hospital, I'm at the end of my rope."

"I understand, Yolanda. I wish there were something more I could do to protect you from the heartache and pain that you're dealing with right now. You're very special to me, and I care for you very much."

Tom embraced me in his arms, held me tight, and kissed me tenderly. *I wish Tom would never let go of me. I feel safe in his arms.*

With my head on his shoulder, I said, "I'm glad we met and I'm looking forward to spending the rest of my life with you."

Tom spoke softly as he held me close and said, "I feel the same way. You're the best thing that ever happened to me, Yolanda."

"You mean the world to me, Tom."

Before leaving to go home, he said, "I'll pick you up tomorrow morning around eight o'clock."

We kissed good night. After he left, I locked the door. *I wish Tom would have stayed with me tonight.*

For some reason, I had the premonition that I shouldn't have been left alone in the motel that night. *Something just doesn't feel right. I'm so afraid without Tom here.*

The bed had loose springs that kept popping up as I tried to relax and get comfortable. I heard people making strange noises outside my window, which was unsettling since my room was at ground level. *I wonder if they saw Tom leave and they know I'm here alone. I feel frightened and helpless.*

I turned on the water faucet in the bathtub full force to drown out the noise. *I can still hear the creepy noises outside. I have to get out of here. I'll never be able to sleep.* I grabbed my things and left the motel immediately.

After leaving, I crossed Queens Boulevard and headed for a diner I could see about a quarter of a mile down the boulevard. I found a phone booth outside the diner. I frantically dialed Tom's phone number a few times and got a busy signal. *His mother must have taken the phone off the hook. What am I going to do? I'm out here all alone.*

The diner was open twenty-four hours. I went inside to the ladies' room and tried to collect my thoughts. Suddenly a scary thought came to mind. *Maybe I'm being followed after what went on at the motel.*

At that point, my goal was to get home as soon as possible. Being determined to get there, I ran out of the diner to stand alongside the boulevard, trying to wave down a car. This was my first experience hitchhiking, and I was paralyzed with fear. *Who knows what kind of maniac could stop and pick me up? Please, God, let me get home safely.*

It appeared that none of the drivers saw me in time to slow down. *Obviously this desperate attempt isn't working. I guess I have no choice but to start walking toward home.*

I figured home was about three miles away. As I walked along a desolate strip of the boulevard, I spotted the Pan Am Hotel up ahead. I decided to stop there and ask someone at the front desk if I could use the phone. The person on duty said it was okay. I called home and Mom picked up the phone. I asked, "Can you and Al pick me up at the Pan Am Hotel right away?"

"Yes, I'll wake up Al and we'll come and get you."

As far as I was concerned, they couldn't get there soon enough. While waiting for them in the lobby, I saw two burly men walking over to lock the front doors from the inside with a key. I was suspicious of the men and felt threatened so I didn't want to hang around. *I have to get out of here now!* I raced out of the motel before they locked the doors, leaving my suitcase behind.

I went back to the boulevard and tried to wave down a car. Eventually, a taxicab stopped and the driver said, "Miss, I'll give you a ride."

I felt relieved at first but after looking into the cab, I noticed that the cab driver's license on display had expired the year before. I said, "No, thanks." *I'm afraid to think what could have happened if I got into the cab with him.*

I continued my efforts to get someone to stop and finally a man pulled up and asked where I needed to go. Afraid that he wouldn't take me all the way home, I lied and told him I had to get to Saint John's Hospital immediately. I reasoned that he would take me to the hospital because it was along the boulevard and not too far from where he picked me up. Even though I wasn't sure what I'd do once he dropped me off, at least I'd be closer to home. After we arrived, I thanked the man. As I walked up the stairs of the hospital, a car pulled up alongside the curb and one of the guys yelled, "There she is!"

Perhaps I should have gone into the hospital, but I panicked and went back to the boulevard and attempted to get another ride. As I was doing this, the two guys kept driving around nearby and shouting obscene remarks at me. I spotted a bus driver parked close by and asked him for a ride. He told me he was at the end of his run and that it was against company rules to take me home. I resumed my efforts to get a ride. Soon after, a man stopped and I told him I worked at the hospital and needed a ride home. He agreed to take me. *What a relief!*

The front door was wide open. Dad stood just outside the door waiting for me to come in. I walked up the steps and greeted him with a kiss on the cheek and went inside.

He said, "Yolanda, I'm glad you got home okay. I love you. Please stay here! Don't leave!"

After all my efforts in trying to get home, which he wasn't aware of, I had no desire to go anywhere. I called Tom, and fortunately this time the phone rang and he picked it up. He asked, "Where are you? Are you all right?"

"I called you earlier but the phone was busy."

"My mom must have taken the phone off the hook before going to bed, which I wasn't aware of. I had trouble sleeping and just got up before you called and put the phone back on the hook."

"Tom, I'm at home. You need to come here right away!"

"I'll get ready and come over."

I felt like an emotional wreck after my disturbing ordeal, starting from the time Tom left me in the motel until I arrived home safely.

Meanwhile, Mom and Al arrived after having looked for me since my call came from the Pan Am Hotel. They brought the suitcase I had left there. Al tried to talk with me and calm me down. I found it difficult to respond to him because I was wound up and exhausted. I just wanted to talk with Tom.

Tom arrived and came into my bedroom where I was lying down. I jumped up when I saw him. We wrapped our arms tightly around each other. Then I closed the door and we sat down on the edge of the bed to talk. I started to tell him what had occurred after he left me at the motel. Within a few minutes, we were interrupted. My mother opened the bedroom door, standing there with two ambulance attendants. Tom and I stood up.

The attendants came into my bedroom, and one of them said, "Your mother called and asked for us to take you to the hospital. She said you need psychiatric care."

"I'm not going anywhere with you. I'm over twenty-one, and you can't force me to go!" They turned around and left.

Mom stood at my open bedroom door with a stern look on her face since she hadn't succeeded in getting me to the hospital. I said, "Mom, last night you came over to Tom's house and insisted I go to the hospital. I went there and got evaluated. The doctor told me I didn't need to be admitted!"

Mom turned around, and I closed the door. I felt relieved that I could finally tell Tom everything that had happened after he had left me at the motel.

Tom said, "I'm angry with myself for leaving you at the motel alone. I can't believe what you've been through. If anything would have happened to you, I could never have forgiven myself. I'm very sorry that because of me you had to go through such a nightmare. Please forgive me."

"I'm not upset with you, Tom. We couldn't have anticipated what was going to happen after you left."

"I guess you're right, but I wish I had stayed with you. Then none of this would have happened." Tom took me in his arms. "I'll never leave you alone like that again under any circumstances. I love you, and I'll always be there for you."

I felt secure in his arms and certain that he was sincere and would keep his word. This assurance was exactly what I needed from him, and it brought me comfort and peace, in spite of the turmoil.

Chapter 9

Tying the Knot

$\mathcal{J}$NITIALLY, I FELT relieved to be back with my family on that Saturday after the ordeal I had gone through trying to get home from the motel. Soon after Tom left my house that morning, I fell asleep and didn't wake up until early afternoon. When I got out of bed and walked into the living room, Mom was sitting on the couch. She looked up and glared at me. In a sharp tone of voice, she said, "Your dad and I decided we're not going to pay for any of the wedding expenses."

"I can't believe what you're telling me, Mom. The wedding is scheduled to take place in two weeks!"

"Well, you can still have the wedding."

"I don't understand. What do you mean?"

"You and Tom will have to pay for it."

"We don't have the money!"

Despair overwhelmed me. I didn't know what else to say. From past experience, I knew that arguing with Mom any further was not going to change her mind. I turned around and rushed back to my bedroom, closed the door, and sat down on my bed. Sharp pains shot through my abdomen, and I choked up with tears. *What are we going to do? Neither Tom nor I have money to pay for a wedding with nearly two hundred guests. I just spent most of my savings on buying a new car.*

After regaining my composure to some extent, I called Tom from the phone in my room and told him the bad news. He responded, "What! Are you serious?"

55

"Yes, I am."

"We can't pay for the wedding, Yolanda."

"I know. At this point, I feel like I'm on the verge of a nervous breakdown."

"I'm very concerned about you."

"Tom, I'm devastated."

"I understand. Can I come over and pick you up? We have to figure out what to do next."

"That's fine. I'll see you soon."

When Tom arrived, I ran out to the car. He drove a few blocks away from my home and parked. He shut off the engine and we talked.

I said, "After what my mom told me about not paying for the wedding, there's no way I can go through with getting married on August 16th like we planned. The stress I'm feeling is unbearable." Tears welled up in my eyes. "I feel like an emotional wreck, and my body is racked with pain. I still haven't gotten over what happened last night—the scene at your house when my mom came over, going to the hospital, and going through what I did to get home from the motel."

Tom reached into his back pocket and took out his handkerchief for me to wipe away the tears. He said, "Yolanda, I know it's been extremely difficult for you over the past four months. You've had to deal with one crushing blow after another, and now this."

"I can't take much more, Tom."

"I want all this heartache in your life to stop and I'll do whatever it takes to make it happen." He took my hand and kissed it gently. "Yolanda, what can we do?"

"The only thing I can think of is to elope."

"I feel terrible that things aren't working out to go through with the wedding."

"Me too, Tom."

"I never imagined we'd have to elope."

"Me neither."

"Do you think there's anything we can do to change your mother's mind?"

"No."

"Well, I guess the only solution is for us to elope, Yolanda."

It was mind-boggling to think through everything and come up with a plan. One thing we knew was that we definitely wanted to get married before moving away from New York. Our original plans were to go to Vermont after the wedding reception, have a short honeymoon there, and then Tom would start his new job assignment.

Tom said, "We'll have to meet with your parish priest as soon as possible."

"You're right. I'll call and set up an appointment to see him early next week."

"When I drop you off at home later, how are you going to avoid getting into a confrontation with your mother?"

"I don't know, but I'll have to stay calm no matter what happens. I don't want her to suspect I'll be leaving home soon."

"How much longer do you think you can deal with living at home?"

"Probably not more than a day or two. That should give me enough time to secretly pack my belongings. When I'm ready to leave, I'll call you to come pick me up."

After Tom took me home, I started packing my two light-blue Samsonite suitcases and concealed them in my bedroom closet. My initials were on each piece of luggage. *These were such a nice gift Mom and Dad gave me years ago. I never thought I'd use them to elope.*

Tom had to get his belongings packed and be ready to leave home on a moment's notice. A few days later, I called him after he got home from work and asked him to pick me up since there was no one at home. I had written a note for my parents that I planned to leave on the kitchen table. It explained that Tom and I were going to elope before Saturday, August 16th. On that day, later in the morning, we'd stop by to see them and say good-bye before leaving for Vermont.

When Tom came over to get me, I asked him, "What was your mother's reaction when you told her about us eloping?"

"I could tell she was disappointed, but she didn't seem too surprised. I mentioned why we couldn't go through with the wedding plans and that we'd be staying at a motel in Queens. She wished us well and didn't ask me any questions. I kissed her good-bye and told her I'd get in touch with her after we got married."

"I'm glad she took it okay."

"I am too, Yolanda."

Tom placed my luggage next to his in the trunk of our car. I went to my bedroom closet and took out the exquisite wedding gown. *I remember the day I first saw this gorgeous gown and selected it, anticipating one of the most important and exciting days of my life.*

My heart was broken, knowing I would never wear the dress on my wedding day. Tears filled my eyes. I carried the gown out to the car and carefully laid it in the trunk on top of the luggage. *I'll never get to wear this beautiful gown.*

Tom had tears in his eyes as he looked at me and the gown. He closed the trunk and we drove away.

That night, we went to a motel at La Guardia Airport, but it was too expensive to stay there more than one night. We moved to another motel in Kew Gardens that was much more reasonable. With the subway located nearby, it was convenient for Tom to commute to work in Manhattan. Our plan was to stay there until we left for Vermont.

I had set up an appointment to see Father Farrell, the priest who was supposed to marry us on August 16th. We met with him and explained why it wouldn't work out to get married on that day and that we needed to elope so we could be married before moving to Vermont. Since he was the lead priest in charge of the parish, Mom must have told him about the things that were going on between us from her viewpoint. In our discussion with Father Farrell, it seemed that he had prior knowledge of conflicting issues between Mom and me. I found it comforting to spend time with him because he was understanding and compassionate.

Before agreeing to marry us, he asked, "Are you both certain about your decision to get married?"

I said, "Yes, I am."

"I am too," Tom said.

It was agreed the ceremony would take place on Tuesday, August 12th, at seven o'clock in the evening. Father Farrell planned to make arrangements for a couple from the church to be our witnesses.

The plan for the day of our elopement was for Tom to go directly to the church by subway after work, and I would drive from the motel to meet him there. I went out shopping that afternoon, and after returning to the motel, I realized that I had left the key in the room. Therefore, it wasn't possible for me to change into the white dress I wanted to wear for the ceremony. It didn't occur to me to ask at the front desk for a spare key because I was in a hurry to meet Tom. As a result, I showed up at the church wearing a short-sleeved, button-down blouse and culottes, which are knee-length women's trousers cut full in the legs to resemble a skirt. It must have looked unusual to Father Farrell and the two witnesses to see Tom in a suit and me in casual attire.

Before we exchanged vows, Father Farrell explained the meaning of commitment in a marriage and the significance of being joined together as a wedded couple. His words were encouraging and meant a lot to us.

After the ceremony, he and the witnesses congratulated us. Although it was a happy occasion and we were thrilled to be married, it was a bittersweet experience. We missed the joy of sharing the moment with family, relatives, and friends.

On Friday night, we went to see Tom's mother. His brother Vin was visiting so we got to spend time with him as well. It was our first contact with relatives after getting married on Tuesday. On Saturday morning at 11 o'clock, we visited my parents, and some relatives were there, including my Uncle Bela from Hungary. He didn't speak English, so Tom couldn't talk with him, but my uncle and I enjoyed a nice conversation. Mom and Dad served lunch and it was good to see everyone. Mom acted as if nothing had happened and everything was fine. Tom and I didn't stay too long because of having to leave for Vermont.

After all the challenges leading up to our marriage, it was such a relief to finally tie the knot.

Chapter 10

Courtroom Drama

(W)E STAYED IN a motel on the outskirts of Brattleboro after arriving in southern Vermont. New Hampshire is east of this town, just across the Connecticut River. To receive our mail, we got a post office box in town, since it was convenient for Tom to stop in Brattleboro daily on his way home from work.

Vermont was rural and quiet compared to the hustle and bustle of New York City. We didn't miss the bumper-to-bumper traffic, blaring car horns, and crowded subways during rush hour.

On bright, sunny days, we enjoyed driving through the countryside. The sunshine intensified the natural beauty of the lush, green meadows and valleys. Streams flowing with crystal clear waters glistened in the sunlight. Tree-covered mountains decorated the landscape. How exhilarating to be surrounded by wide open spaces.

It was a delight to see horses grazing in the grassy meadows as we drove on winding, two-lane country roads. At times, we felt compelled to pull off the road and get out of the car to admire horses up close. One day, as we stood in front of a wooden fence and watched four horses about fifty feet away, they walked over to where we stood and hung their heads over the fence. What a thrill to reach out and gently stroke their faces. We fed them handfuls of grass gathered from alongside the road. It was breathtaking to interact with these majestic creatures. Back in New York, the horses we saw were ridden by police officers on patrol, and people weren't allowed to get near them.

In Brattleboro, most of the stores were closed by five o'clock. By early evening the town looked deserted. Friday night was the exception, when the stores stayed open until nine o'clock. Tom and I were amazed to see a hardware store that regularly left many of its wares outside in front of the store overnight after closing, which is something we had never seen. In New York City, if a store left any merchandise outdoors overnight, it would have been stolen by morning.

I loved Vermont. It was such a quiet and peaceful place to live. I was glad we had moved there after getting married. We looked forward to leaving behind the problems and challenges leading up to our marriage.

When Tom left for work in the morning, I stayed at the motel since we had only one car. There were no stores within walking distance. This time alone was a good opportunity for me to relax and get some much-needed rest.

We had been in Vermont about three weeks. After Tom left for work one morning, I could never have anticipated how my life was about to spiral out of control.

The special delivery letter from my mother traumatized me because of her harsh and angry words. All the anguish leading up to our elopement came rushing back. I couldn't hold back the tears. My mind was a blur and I couldn't think rationally. Paranoia seized me when a group of boisterous teenagers rented the room next door. I became unnerved, thinking they might be watching me through a two-way mirror in the bathroom. To make sure they couldn't see me, I hung towels over the light fixture above the mirror. Events that followed led to my arrest for starting a fire in our motel bathroom. Next, I found myself behind bars.

Just before I went to sleep that night in jail, Tom arrived and was given permission to see me. When I saw him, I jumped up from the cold metal folding chair. *What a relief to see Tom. I wish he could take me away from this awful place.* I walked over to him. As I stood inside the cell door with tears in my eyes, he reached through the bars and held my hands. *How comforting it feels just to hold his hands. I wish he could wrap his arms around me.*

Looking at me tenderly with tears welling up in his eyes, he asked softly, "How are you holding up?"

"I have a splitting headache. I feel nauseated, and my body aches after such a horrible day."

"I understand, with what you've been through."

"Right now I just want to sleep, but there are spiders all over the jail cell, and you know how terrified I am of spiders! My mind is racing. I can't think straight. I can't settle myself down, because I don't know what's going to happen next. I want to get out of here and be with you again."

"I know, Yolanda. I wish I could do more to help you."

"Did you find a lawyer?" I asked anxiously.

"Yes."

"Thank God." *What a relief. Maybe there's hope of being back with Tom again soon.*

"I used the Yellow Pages and found a lawyer. I told him it was urgent that I see him because you're in jail. He said he'd see me right away. I went to his office and explained what happened to you. He agreed to represent you. He'll talk with you in court tomorrow morning before the judge starts the proceedings."

"Okay. I'm exhausted. I need to try and get some sleep."

Still holding my hands, Tom said, "I love you, Yolanda. I'll see you tomorrow. I hope you can sleep tonight and that you'll feel better in the morning."

"Me too. I'll see you in court. I love you."

We kissed good-bye. My heart sank as I watched Tom leave. *I wish he could take me with him. I've never felt more alone.*

Throughout the night I tossed and turned. I was panic-stricken at the thought of big, black spiders coming anywhere near me or crawling on me. The cot in the jail cell had a lumpy mattress about two inches thick. I couldn't get comfortable. By morning, I was sick to my stomach. My head still throbbed from the night before. I had chills from sweating all night long. *I hardly slept. I feel miserable.*

I desperately wanted to take a shower, but the jail didn't have one. I had on the T-shirt and shorts from the previous day, which I had slept in overnight. *I can't believe there's no shower. I wish I at least had a change of clothes.*

Someone brought me breakfast. I had no appetite and refused the meal. My life had gone haywire. Prior to the fire, I had my freedom. Now I was in jail waiting to go before a judge.

Two police officers took me from jail to the courthouse. Tom stood in the lobby dressed in a light blue pin-striped suit. *He looks so handsome.*

We approached each other, and without saying anything, we gave each other a brief, gentle hug and kiss. *I can't wait until this is over and we're back together again.*

Standing nearby was my lawyer. Tom introduced him to me as Mr. Burke. We only had a few minutes to talk before the court hearing was scheduled to start. With the chaotic events leading up to this point, I couldn't collect my thoughts, much less communicate anything to the attorney about what led to the fire. He didn't ask me any questions. I remember Mr. Burke saying to me, "I don't want you to speak during the hearing. Let me do all the talking."

Shortly after the court proceedings began, the judge allowed Mr. Burke to speak in my defense. He attempted to convince the judge that I had no reason to deliberately start the fire. He argued that I was a person of good character, based on the fact that I was a pharmacist, had no prior police record, and that I was a newlywed of only three weeks. Neither Tom nor I can remember anything else he said on my behalf.

How can he defend me properly? He doesn't know any of the facts that led to the fire. I never got a chance to tell him. I never got to tell Tom either. I just want to leave this place and be back with Tom.

The judge looked at Mr. Burke in disbelief as he listened to him. It appeared he wasn't impressed with what he heard. After Mr. Burke's closing comments, there was silence for a few moments. Suddenly, the judge, eyes bulging and his face fiery red with anger, blurted out in a loud, angry tone, "I'm not convinced your client is innocent, and I order her to be committed to the local mental health hospital!"

I looked at Tom. Tears welled up in my eyes and his. *Is this really happening? I don't want to be separated from Tom. My heart is pounding so hard it feels like it's going to come out of my chest. I'm scared. What's going to happen next?*

Two police officers took me to the hospital immediately after the hearing. Tom followed in our car, and when we got there he watched as the police escorted me into the building. They took me to be evaluated by a psychiatrist. After spending time asking me questions, he concluded I didn't need to be admitted. *What a relief! I can't wait until Tom finds out!*

The police walked me outside where Tom was waiting. I said to him, "The psychiatrist evaluated me and told me I don't need to be admitted."

Tom's face lit up. "That's great news."

Back I went with the police to the courthouse to see the judge. Tom followed us.

When the judge found out I wasn't admitted, he was furious and shouted, "I'm going to call the hospital and straighten this out!" He ordered the police, "Take her back to the hospital!" He glared at me, "You'll be admitted this time!"

I can't believe this is happening. What a nasty judge. I don't want to be put in the hospital and separated from Tom. The doctor said I didn't need to be there.

The police took me back and the same psychiatrist did another evaluation. This time he said I had to be admitted. Clearly, the judge's influence had played a significant part in changing his mind. It was devastating for us as newlyweds to realize we would not only be separated, but also that we had no idea how long I would be required to stay at the hospital.

Tom stayed with me during the admission process. The administrator introduced himself as Mr. Williams. He asked Tom to sign me in, which was quite unexpected. I spoke up right away and told Tom not to do it. He agreed. Mr. Williams continued to pursue the issue, but there was nothing he could say to change our minds. If Tom had signed me in, he would have been obligated to pay for charges incurred while I remained there. The judge's decision resulted in my placement at the hospital. Therefore, Tom and I were certain the state was responsible for paying all bills.

The day after my admission, Tom came to visit me. It was the first chance we got to discuss how the fire had started. I told him about the disturbing letter from my mother and the obnoxious teenagers next door.

I said, "After reading the letter, I felt like an emotional wreck. Then I started feeling paranoid that the teenagers may be looking at me through a two-way mirror in the bathroom. I hung towels on the light fixture above the sink in the bathroom to cover the mirror."

Tom said, "It's obvious to me the heat from the light bulbs caused the towels to catch fire. When the towels around the light fixture burned, they fell into the sink, which made it look like that's where the fire started. When the fireman took me into the bathroom and showed me the burnt towels piled up in the sink, he told me you started the fire there. I didn't know what to think, but it didn't make any sense that you purposely started the fire."

"I'm relieved you know what really happened, Tom."

"I'll let Mr. Burke know the fire was just an accident. Maybe he can get you out of here right way."

I looked at Tom, smiled, and breathed a sigh of relief. "I can't wait to get out of the hospital and be back with you."

"I want you out of this place, Yolanda. Hopefully it will happen soon."

When Tom went back to the motel room, he saw black burn marks on the wall only around the light fixture, which proved that was where the fire had started. He called Mr. Burke and informed him of what actually had occurred. Next, Tom took photographs of the wall and fixture and had them developed.

The pictures proved the fire started around the light fixture. After showing them to Mr. Burke, he agreed the fire was accidental. However, he couldn't obtain an immediate release to get me out of the hospital. A follow-up hearing had to be scheduled. Additionally, Mr. Burke wanted to make sure a different judge would hear the case, since the first one was unreasonable and difficult to deal with.

Chapter 11

Depressing Place

*T*HE DAY AFTER Tom's first visit to the hospital was an extra difficult one for me. When I woke up that morning, the sun shone
brightly through the window. I remained in the twin-sized bed a few
minutes, covered with a top sheet and lightweight blanket. *What am I
doing here?*

I sat up and looked around the room. It had only a four-drawer, walnut
dresser along with the bed. Nothing hung on the dreary, white walls. I
stood up, walked to the window, and gazed out at the hospital grounds.

My mind swirled with thoughts. *Is this really happening? I can't believe
I'm separated from Tom. I miss him more than I could ever have imagined.
God, please help me get through this.*

The reality of my circumstances struck me head-on. I was overcome
with loneliness and started to daydream. *I never expected anything like
this to happen to me after Tom and I got married. I wish he were here right
now holding me in his arms.*

A piercing ache went through my chest and stomach, and it lingered
the rest of the day until Tom's visit. I sat in the lobby late that afternoon
and couldn't wait for his arrival after work. I picked up a magazine from
the table next to me and tried to focus on it to make the time pass more
quickly. I couldn't concentrate. I looked at the door, waiting for my dear
husband. When he got there, I jumped out of my seat and ran to meet
him. We embraced, held each other tight, and kissed.

"I've been looking forward to seeing you all day, Tom."

"I've been looking forward to seeing you too."

We went to the cafeteria to have dinner and afterwards enjoyed a long, relaxing walk outside on the hospital grounds.

As we leisurely walked hand in hand, I said, "I can't wait to get out of this depressing place."

"I know, but you have to be patient and try to take one day at a time. At this point, it's impossible to figure out when you'll get out of here."

"You're right. I'm hoping it'll be sooner than later."

"Me too, Yolanda." Tom stopped walking, turned to me, and swept me into his arms. We kissed tenderly. He continued, "I love you, and I'll do whatever I can to be supportive and help you get through this tough time."

"I appreciate everything you're doing," I replied with tears in my eyes. "Just being together now means so much to me." Tom took out his handkerchief and wiped the tears from my eyes.

"Yolanda, I can't put into words how much I miss you."

"I feel the same, Tom." We kissed again and resumed our walk.

"After we got married and moved to Vermont, I thought we'd have a fresh start and could put all the past problems behind us, Yolanda. I never expected us to be separated like this."

"Me neither. I looked forward to leaving New York and enjoying a peaceful life in Vermont with you. Now, I'm stuck at this hospital."

"I wish I could take you away from here tonight."

"I wish you could."

"How did your day go, Yolanda?"

"Not well. I can't stop thinking about how I ended up here. The trauma that started in New York has followed me to Vermont and it seems never-ending."

"Is there anything I can do to help you feel better?"

We stopped and looked at each other. "One thing you can do is take me in your arms and hold me."

My darling husband wrapped his arms around me. I held on to him as tightly as I could and buried my face against his chest. *I wish he would never let me go. His strong, muscular arms make me feel secure.*

Tom whispered in my ear, "I love you very much, Yolanda."

"Being in your arms and hearing you tell me how much you care means so much to me. Your love and support give me the strength to believe I'll get through this and we'll be back together again."

Tom stayed with me until visiting hours were over at eight o'clock. Typically, this was our routine during the week and the highlight of my day. I appreciated the time Tom spent listening to what I shared about my feelings and experiences from day to day.

I felt better emotionally and physically whenever I saw Tom and spent time with him. He was my only lifeline to the outside world. I yearned to be with him each day. Weekends were extra special because we could spend more time together. His visits and encouraging words helped me cope with the situation.

Tom and I had decided not to tell relatives or friends about this ordeal. We felt it was a private part of our lives. As far as they knew, everything was fine with us.

My level of anxiety remained high throughout most of my stay at the hospital. I felt I didn't belong there. I thought about how much I wanted to be free and as far away from that place as possible. I hated being confined, especially not knowing when I would be released and reunited with Tom.

I never got adjusted to being separated from him and the outside world. However, I was grateful to have unrestricted privileges to come and go from my private room and walk around on the hospital grounds between 8:00 A.M. and 8:00 P.M. Even though the hospital wasn't the same as jail, I felt that remaining there against my will was similar to being locked up behind bars.

The hospital grounds included various buildings, some of which had patients in locked wards. One day as I leisurely walked toward one of the buildings, I heard people inside the wards screaming and howling like dogs. *What frightful sounds. How terrifying.*

I turned around and quickly walked in the opposite direction. *I can't wait to get out of this dismal place. I'll never go near that building again.*

During my stay at the hospital, I was required to attend two group therapy sessions weekly, one led by a psychiatrist and the other by a psychologist. The psychiatrist, Dr. Turner, led one of the sessions. He took part in having me admitted to the hospital when I came from the courthouse to be evaluated. For that reason, I disliked him and made it a point to steer clear of him outside the mandatory therapy sessions.

In the sessions, different topics were brought up, and anyone was free to contribute to the discussions. Initially I kept silent and listened to what others had to say. I felt resentful about my circumstances and had no interest in saying anything. However, after a few sessions, I decided to open up and share some of my thoughts. I realized that participating in the group discussions would likely be a positive factor in getting me released from the hospital.

In addition to the therapy sessions, I met with a social worker, Judy, three times a week. My sessions were positive and enjoyable, and I found her to be compassionate and friendly. She made me feel at ease when I shared my feelings. I felt comfortable telling her what had happened leading up to Tom's and my eloping, how the motel fire had started, and how I had ended up in the hospital.

During one of our sessions, Judy said, "I can understand why you were under such an enormous amount of stress leading up to the fire."

"I appreciate being able to talk with you. You're sympathetic and kind."

"I'm glad I can be of help, Yolanda. I have something in mind I think you would enjoy and find relaxing. It's a ceramics class where you can make ornamental items. It should be a pleasant activity and help pass some of the time while you're here."

"That sounds like a good idea. I'd like to give it a try."

When I went to the class, I decided to make Tom a green turtle and a brown squirrel, each no bigger than the palm of his hands. It was fun making them. The teacher said, "You did a great job, Yolanda. They came out perfect."

"Thank you. I'm glad Judy encouraged me to take your class." *I can't wait to give them to Tom.*

That evening when Tom came to visit me after work, I met him on the hospital grounds with my hands behind my back. As he walked toward me, I said, "Sweetheart, I have two handmade surprises for you."

He grinned. His eyes lit up with excitement. "Show me, I can't wait to see them."

"Close your eyes, stretch out your arms, and open your hands."

I placed the squirrel in one of Tom's hands and the turtle in the other. *I can't wait to see his reaction.*

"Now open your eyes."

"Wow! They're beautiful. You did such a great job, Yolanda. It was thoughtful of you to make them for me. Thanks a lot."

"You're welcome. Be careful. They're fragile."

"Okay."

While Tom held the precious little critters in his hands, he wrapped his arms around me tightly and we kissed. What a wonderful start to that evening's visit!

Tom ate meals with me in the hospital cafeteria whenever possible. During the week when he came right after work, we had supper. On weekends, we usually enjoyed lunch and supper together. At first, Tom wasn't charged for meals. After a week, the hospital administrator, Mr. Williams, decided that he should pay one dollar for each meal. Tom agreed and thought it was quite a bargain.

One sunny day as I was sitting on a bench and reading a book on the hospital grounds, Tom sneaked up behind me and said, "Hi, Yolanda."

That's Tom! I jumped up, turned around, and said, "What a great surprise! I'm thrilled to see you earlier than usual."

"I got out of work early today. I wanted to spend a few extra hours with you."

"That's fantastic!" *I'm so excited.*

We embraced. *I don't want to let go of him.*

We kissed a few times and he said, "How's your day going, Yolanda?"

"Much better since you're here. Let's walk over to the building that has a piano. You haven't played for awhile. At this time of the day, there shouldn't be anyone playing the piano."

"Sounds good."

We walked into the building. Tom sat down on the piano bench and I stood beside him. He played some of my favorite songs. The last one, by Nat King Cole, was, "When I Fall in Love." After he finished playing, I said, "That song is special to me, Tom. It reminds me of our love for each other."

"I enjoyed playing for you. Maybe someday we'll buy a piano."

"That would be wonderful, Tom."

"Yolanda, let's go outside and walk to the wooded area at the edge of the hospital grounds. We haven't been back there yet."

"Okay." *I love our walks together.*

We held hands and strolled there. One tree caught Tom's attention. It had smooth bark. He said, "I'd like to carve something for you on this tree with my pocket knife. I don't want you to see it until it's done. It'll be a surprise."

"I can't wait to see it."

"Yolanda, would you please go and sit on that bench and promise me you won't peek?"

"Okay." *I wonder what Tom's up to.*

"I'll let you know when I'm finished."

After about twenty minutes, Tom came over, looked at me with a smile, and took my hands in his. I stood up. He said, "I'm done. Let me show you what I did."

We walked side by side to the tree with our arms around each other.

I exclaimed, "Tom, I love your masterpiece!" *How romantic of him to carve TB loves YB with a heart-shaped border.*

"I'm glad you like it."

Tom and I stood there a few minutes admiring the carving. We hugged and kissed. *I wish this moment could last forever.*

We happily walked away hand in hand. Although we were apart overnight, we spent precious moments together daily. Our love and commitment as a couple deepened.

I was fortunate to have a private room for the first three weeks at the hospital. Whenever Mr. Williams saw Tom, he hounded him to pay bills incurred for my stay there. Tom stood his ground and refused to accommodate the man because the state was responsible for my admission. Repeatedly explaining this to Mr. Williams left Tom increasingly aggravated, since the man wouldn't stop harassing him. Bills began arriving at Tom's workplace, but this tactic proved unsuccessful. Mr. Williams must have finally realized that he wasn't going to get any money from us. Consequently, I suddenly got transferred from the private room to a ward where there were about twenty women.

What a drastic change. My private room had been located in a part of the hospital complex that was peaceful and quiet. In comparison, the ward was an open, noisy area with beds lined up on both sides of the room. The beds were no more than a few feet apart. I went from having my own dresser to sharing one with someone else.

Some nights in the ward were disturbing. Occasionally, patients woke up screaming in the middle of the night. I hated the ward but made the best of it, since I only had to sleep there at night.

I got to know a thirty-year-old lady in the bed next to mine. We enjoyed talking before going to sleep. She had a darling picture of her two children on the dresser we shared. A few days after I got to know her, she was transferred to another building. She accidentally took some of my clothes from the dresser. After finding my things missing, I told the person in charge of the ward. She escorted me to the building where the other lady was staying to retrieve my belongings. This location was obviously for those with more serious problems because the patients were behind locked doors.

Two weeks after my admission to the hospital, I made an appointment with Dr. Turner. I had come to the conclusion that confiding in him would be in my best interest to get released from the hospital. I shared what happened before getting married and what transpired leading up to the fire in the motel. He replied, "I'm going to schedule a committee of mental health professionals to hear your case."

When the day arrived, Dr. Turner and I went into a room where five committee members were sitting at a table. He introduced me, and we sat at the table across from them. They asked me about the specific problems and circumstances I had been dealing with prior to the fire. I felt knots in my stomach during the meeting, knowing that my release depended on the conclusions reached by the group. I explained what happened leading up to Tom's and my eloping in New York and the events just prior to the motel fire. Basically I told the committee the same facts I had shared with Dr. Turner.

The next day, I had an appointment with Dr. Turner. He smiled and said, "Yolanda, you'll be happy to hear that the outcome of the committee meeting is in your favor. I'll contact your lawyer, Mr. Burke, so he can schedule a court hearing."

"I appreciate what you've done to help me. Thank you." I felt elated. *I can't wait to tell Tom.*

When he came to visit me later that afternoon, I said, "I've got great news, Tom."

"What is it?"

"Dr. Turner told me the outcome of the committee meeting was in my favor. He's going to contact Mr. Burke to have him schedule a court hearing."

Tom's eyes lit up. He put his hands on my shoulders and I grabbed his waist. "What fantastic news, Yolanda. I'm sure you'll be out of here soon." He pulled me toward him and gave me a bear hug. After several moments, he released me. I looked at Tom, he looked at me, and then our lips met.

"I can't wait to leave the hospital and start a new life with you, Tom. It'll be wonderful being back together."

"That's for sure. Let's go to the cafeteria, have supper, and take a long walk."

"Sounds good, Tom."

When it came to the day of the hearing, it was a tremendous relief to see another judge and not the nasty one that had me admitted to the hospital. Soon after the new judge started the proceedings, it was obvious he was sympathetic toward me. Dr. Turner provided a written statement of testimony on my behalf. It clarified that I could not be held responsible for the fire, since it was not started intentionally. Also, his statement indicated that I was a victim of circumstances and under intense emotional stress prior to and at the time of the fire.

The judge dropped the arson charge that was pronounced against me at the first hearing. As far as monetary responsibilities, the only bills we owed were to Mr. Burke for his services and less than a hundred dollars to the motel owner to cover repair of the minor damage caused by the fire.

During his final statement, the judge smiled at Tom and me and said, "I'm sure it's been difficult for you to be separated four and a half weeks, especially after being married only a short time. I'm happy to see you reunited. Now you can go on with your lives."

Tom and I walked out of the courthouse holding hands. Just outside the door of the building, we embraced and kissed. *The torture of being apart from my husband is finally over.*

On the way to our car, I turned to look at Tom and we stopped walking. With tears of joy, I said, "I'm thrilled to be free at last and back together with you."

Tom pulled me into his arms and held me tight. With his cheek pressed against mine, he replied, "After being separated and all you've been through, I'm ecstatic that we're finally reunited, Yolanda."

Tom opened the driver side door, and I slid to the center of the black vinyl bench seat so I'd be right beside him when he got in. I loved sitting close to Tom.

After getting into the car, Tom said, "Let's go to the hospital and pick up your belongings. Then I'll take you to the place where we'll be living. I'm sure you'll like it."

"I can't wait to see it!"

Chapter 12

Fresh Start

*W*HILE I WAS in the hospital, Tom had looked in the local newspaper for a place to rent. After a phone call with a lady about her ad, he went to see the rental property. It was a travel trailer, eight feet wide by thirty-five feet long, on an acre of land located a few miles outside of the town of Putney, Vermont. Tom liked it at first sight. When he found out the rent was only seventy-five dollars a month and there was no lease, he didn't hesitate to take it. He had moved from the motel to the trailer two weeks prior to my release from the hospital.

As we drove up the road and approached the trailer, I said, "This is such a beautiful rural area."

After Tom stepped out of the car, I slid toward him and got out. We stood side by side in the driveway, our arms tightly around each other. I thought, *It feels wonderful standing here with my dear husband. I'm more than ready to start a new chapter in my life.*

As we gazed across the road, I took a few deep breaths of fresh, country air. "What a magnificent view from our front yard. The green valley with hills behind it looks prettier than a postcard."

"It does, Yolanda."

"Tom, aren't those trees up on the hills beautiful with the orange, gold, and cranberry-colored autumn leaves?"

"Yes, especially with the sunshine and clear blue sky."

"And look at the cows grazing in the meadow."

"Yolanda, this is such a peaceful place."

"It is. I know I'm going to enjoy living here."

"Me too." We looked at each other and kissed. Tom continued, "Let me show you the trailer."

We turned around and walked hand in hand slowly up the driveway. *I'm so excited.*

The faded blue trailer rested on a concrete block foundation. "I can't wait to see it. I've never been in one before, Tom."

"It's small but cozy."

"I'm sure this will be like paradise compared to my hospital stay."

Tom smiled, nodded in agreement, and said, "Look at this screened-in front porch that's almost as long as the trailer. We can store some of our things out here."

"You're right."

A white wooden stairway with eight steps and a railing led up from the crushed stone driveway to the porch. We walked up the stairs, and Tom held the screen door open for me. Approximately ten feet inside the porch, on the left, I saw the door to the trailer.

As we walked in, Tom asked, "What do you think of the honey-colored wood veneer on the walls and ceiling?"

"It's bright and cheerful with the high gloss finish. Is it throughout the place?"

"Yes."

"The red and green plaid couch is charming." I sat on it. "This is comfortable."

"Look at the dining table, Yolanda. It expands into the living room." Tom pulled it open all the way.

"What a long, narrow table." I got up off the couch, walked into the kitchen, and said, "This is cute. I see the sink, but where's the stove, Tom?"

"It's covered with this laminated countertop. To use the stove, the hinged countertop has to be lifted up from the front and pushed to a locked, vertical position against the back wall." Tom showed me how to do it.

"That's neat." I put the countertop up and down a few times.

Next, I followed Tom down the short hallway to the bathroom. "Look at these two sliding doors, one on the kitchen and one on the bedroom side of the bathroom," he said. As we stood inside, he slid each door closed.

"It's private in here with both doors closed," I said. "It's hard to believe that the toilet, sink, and shower fit in this small space."

Tom opened the sliding door to the bedroom. The full-size bed and dresser barely fit inside the room. I sat on the bed, looked up at him, and said, "Sweetheart, I know we'll enjoy living here."

After the tour, we sat down on the couch. Tom looked at me with a grin and said, "I'm happy you like the place, Yolanda."

"I love it! I'm thrilled you found it. What a marvelous fresh start after being in the hospital."

"That's for sure."

"Tom, I can't wait to use this cute little kitchen and make some of your favorite meals. I know how much you love my mom's fried chicken, potato salad, and lemon meringue pie."

"Yes, I do. I know you'll be a terrific cook."

"Let's go shopping at Super Duper's Market in Brattleboro. Then I'll be prepared to make the meal for supper tomorrow night."

"Sounds good, Yolanda!"

The next evening when Tom got home from work, he said, "The fried chicken smells delicious. I can't wait to have it."

"It'll be ready in five minutes. Please light the candles on the table."

"Okay. This is our first candlelight dinner since we've been married."

"Yes, it is," I smiled. *This is going to be romantic.*

I thought the meal turned out perfect and couldn't wait to see Tom's reaction. Soon after we sat down at the table and started eating, Tom raved.

"Everything is outstanding, Yolanda. The chicken is tender and juicy. The crispy breading has a great flavor. The potato salad is scrumptious and goes well with the chicken."

"I'm happy you like my cooking."

"I love your cooking. What a fantastic meal!"

"Thank you." I got up and walked a few steps into the kitchen to bring dessert to the table.

When Tom tasted it, he said, "Wow! Your lemon meringue pie is out of this world." He gobbled it down.

"I'm delighted you're enjoying it."

"I am, very much. Can I please have another piece?"

"Sure. I'll put it on your plate."

"Thanks, Yolanda." He ate the second piece much more slowly.

While I cleaned up after dinner, Tom sat on the couch to rest after a busy day at work. I noticed him reaching toward our stereo record player on a nearby table. He said, "I'm putting on your favorite album, the one I gave you for your birthday, three months after we met."

"That's great." The album included "This Guy's in Love with You," which was one of my favorite songs at the time.

"Do you remember how excited you were, Yolanda, when I gave you the album?"

"You bet I do!" When I heard the song playing, I yelled to Tom from the kitchen, "I'll be there as soon as I finish up."

"Do you want to dance when you're done?"

"Yes, I'd love to, Tom."

It was the most relaxing evening we had spent together since getting married and moving to Vermont. Tom and I were overjoyed to be together again in a place that seemed just right for us at the time.

There were only three homes visible from the trailer, two of which stood way up on the hill behind us. A wooden cabin was on the opposite side of our driveway, only a stone's throw away. According to our landlady, Linnie, an eighty-year-old man lived there.

One day while Tom was at work, I went to the cabin to meet our next-door neighbor. There was no bell so I knocked on the front door. After a few moments I heard him ask, "Who is it?"

"I'm your new next-door neighbor. I'd like to meet you."

The door creaked as it opened. He said, "Hello, I'm Mr. Holt."

"Hi, I'm Yolanda. My husband, Tom, and I moved into the trailer last week. He works at the nuclear power plant construction site near Brattleboro. We moved to Vermont from New York City."

"Come in," he said with a smile.

We stood inside and talked for a few minutes. As I glanced around, I noticed the one-room cabin included a bed, a table, a kitchen with a wood stove, and a sitting area. There appeared to be a bathroom enclosed in one corner of the room. I had never seen a home like that before.

Mr. Holt was thin, frail-looking, and about six feet tall. He seemed pleased I had come over. I enjoyed my short visit. Before I left, he said, "Come back again sometime, and bring your husband. I'd like to meet him."

"Okay. It was a pleasure to meet you, Mr. Holt."

"It was nice to meet you, Yolanda."

Whenever I prepared fried chicken, I took some to Mr. Holt. On occasion Tom came with me. Mr. Holt always smiled and said, "I love your chicken. Thanks for thinking of me."

After we got settled and experienced a taste of country living for about two weeks, our first company from New York visited on a Saturday in October. They planned to stay overnight at a motel before heading home on Sunday.

Before their visit, Tom and I agreed not to bring up anything regarding what had happened to me after we moved to Vermont.

We eagerly awaited their arrival that Saturday morning. They pulled into the driveway honking the horn, and we ran out to meet them. It was wonderful seeing Tom's mother, his sister Nina, her husband Artie, and their dear children, Arthur and Lorraine, fourteen and eleven years old. We cheerfully greeted one another, and many kisses were exchanged. They also brought Trixie, their cute, short-haired, mixed-breed dog. She ran around barking excitedly.

Tom's mom brought one of her homemade Italian specialties, a stuffed pizza large enough to feed everyone. It was in the shape of a horseshoe, filled with ham, Genoa salami, mozzarella, and parmesan cheese. When I saw it, I exclaimed, "Mom, thanks very much for bringing the stuffed pizza. What a surprise! You know how much Tom and I love it."

"You're welcome. I knew you both would enjoy it," she replied with a big smile.

We went inside, sat down in the living room, and talked while my fried chicken was cooking. I had prepared potato salad and lemon meringue pie the night before.

Tom said, "I wish it had been sunny today. You can't appreciate the beautiful scenery with the clouds and rain. On a clear day, the view across the road is spectacular, especially at this time of year when the autumn leaves are bright and colorful."

"It doesn't matter. We're just happy to be here with you," Artie replied.

"That's right," Nina said. "I've missed you a lot. We haven't seen you for almost three months. I wish you didn't live far away." She gave Tom and me each a hug.

Tom looked at his sister tenderly and kissed her on the cheek. Then he looked at everyone else and said, "It's great being together. We've missed all of you."

"I've missed you, Uncle Tom and Aunt Yolanda," Arthur said.

"I've missed you both too," Lorraine chimed in.

Tom's mother choked up with tears. Tom walked over to her, kissed her, and said, "I love you, Mom. I'm so glad you're here."

"I'm happy we could be together," she replied.

"Me too, Mom."

When everything was ready, we sat at the fully-extended dining table. Everybody expressed how much they enjoyed Mom's delicious pizza and the food I prepared.

After the meal, we drove around the countryside in two cars and stopped at gift shops. Before we knew it, the day had ended. We all shed a few tears while saying goodbye. As Tom and I stood in the driveway, our visitors got into the car and backed down onto the road. We waved to each other and Artie honked the horn a few times as they drove away. In a few moments, their car vanished from sight.

As we walked slowly back up the driveway hand in hand, Tom said, "I'm glad they came to see us."

"I am too."

"We had such a great time."

"Yes, we did, Tom. I'm looking forward to the next time we see them."

"Me too, Yolanda."

Chapter 13

Unexpected Visit

$\mathcal{T}$HE WEEK AFTER Tom's relatives visited, I received a phone call from my mother. It took me totally by surprise because I had never given Mom our phone number. She must have gotten it from Tom's mother. I hadn't talked with my mom or dad since Tom and I had left New York two months earlier.

"How are you and Dad?" I asked.

"Okay."

"How are you and Tom doing?"

"Fine."

"That's good. Dad and I want to visit you. We would come by bus on a Saturday and stay a few hours before going back to New York. You won't need to prepare a meal. I'll bring something that I know you and Tom will like."

"I'll talk with Tom and get back to you."

"Okay, Yolanda. Goodbye."

"Bye, Mom."

When I got off the phone, I felt extremely tense. Thoughts about conflicts with my mother flooded my mind. *She called my boss and told her I needed psychiatric care. She tried to get me admitted to the hospital several times. The harsh letter I got from her before the motel fire made me feel like an emotional wreck.*

I sat on the couch quietly for a few minutes, trying to regain my composure. In spite of the problems I had with my mother, I still felt a deep love for her. The pull on my heartstrings brought tears to my eyes. *I don't want the past to come between Mom and me. I just want to have a pleasant relationship with her.*

I called Tom at work and told him about the phone call. He asked, "How did the conversation go?"

"Okay."

"Did she bring up anything from the past?"

"No. She seemed excited about visiting us with my dad."

"When I get home after work, we can pick a date for their visit. See you later, Yolanda. I love you."

"I love you, Tom. Bye."

I felt less tense after talking with Tom. He had always been supportive, no matter what I'd been through before and after we got married. *Thank you, God, for bringing him into my life.*

That night after dinner, Tom and I chose a Saturday in November for my parents to visit. The next day, I called Mom and she agreed the date would be fine.

A whirlwind of emotions plagued me soon after I got off the phone with Mom. Fear crept into my mind and paralyzed me. I felt a chill go through my body. *I want to see Mom and Dad, but I'm afraid Mom and I will get into a confrontation. What am I going to do if that happens during their visit? How will Tom and I handle it?*

That evening while having supper, I told Tom about the gamut of emotions that were haunting me. We stopped eating. He looked at me compassionately with his soothing brown eyes. His love and concern came across before he even said a word. He reached across the table and took my hands in his.

With a soft voice, he said, "Yolanda, please don't worry. Try to stay calm. Since we're married now, I don't think your mother will bring up anything about what happened in New York. If something should come up, I'm here to support you one hundred percent."

Tom's reassuring words were exactly what I needed to hear. Feeling calmer, I replied, "Thank you."

"Yolanda, I also feel some apprehension about their visit, but I'm not going to dwell on it. Let's try to focus on having a relaxing and peaceful time with them. I'm sure the hours we spend together will fly by."

"You're right. I feel better. Talking with you has helped me a lot."

The night before my parents arrived, my emotions got the best of me again. As I stood in the kitchen cleaning up after dinner and Tom was sitting on the couch, I blurted out, "I'm still afraid that things may not go well when my parents are here."

Tom got up, came over to me, and held me gently in his arms. He took my hand and walked me into the living room. We sat down facing one another.

I said, "I'm trying to stay calm, but I can't help feeling uneasy about tomorrow."

"I know, Yolanda. I'm feeling the same way. Hopefully everything will work out okay."

"I didn't realize you were having similar thoughts."

"I am, but I'm determined to remain positive. All we can do is be kind and loving toward them and hope for the best."

"You're right. Thanks for being honest about your feelings. I appreciate the love and support you've given me since we met. I love you."

Tom leaned toward me and we kissed tenderly. Then he whispered in my ear, "I love you very much, Yolanda. Let's go to bed early tonight."

"Okay."

The next day, Saturday, I woke up after a good night's sleep, refreshed and much more prepared to see my parents.

After a delicious mid-morning breakfast of bacon and eggs with buttered toast and fresh coffee, we showered and got ready to go to the bus station. While walking to the car, I said, "What a beautiful autumn day."

"It is, Yolanda. I love chilly days like this, with the sun shining and the clear, blue sky."

"Me too. The weather is perfect."

The bus station was on the outskirts of Brattleboro. As we drove there, neither of us said much. I just enjoyed the scenery. *I hope this day goes well with my parents,* I thought.

We got there, parked, and sat in the car waiting for the bus. Within five minutes, the bus pulled into the station and we got out of the car to greet my parents.

As Tom and I walked to the bus, Mom stepped off with Dad behind her. "We're happy to see you," she smiled and said. Dad nodded in agreement.

"It's nice to see you too," I replied. I kissed each of them on the cheek.

"Hello, Mr. and Mrs. Gyuricza," Tom said. He kissed my mom, and he and my dad shook hands.

I couldn't help but notice Dad carrying something that looked heavy in a sturdy cloth shopping bag. "What do you have in there, Dad?" I asked.

Before he could answer, Mom replied, "I made a big pot of stuffed cabbage for you and Tom. I know it's one of your favorites, Yolanda."

"Yes, it is Mom. I can't wait to eat it."

"There's plenty of it. Whatever we don't finish today, you and Tom can enjoy for leftovers."

"Thanks, Mom, for making it, and thanks, Dad, for carrying it all the way from home."

"Thank you, Mr. and Mrs. Gyuricza."

"You're welcome," Mom and Dad replied in unison.

"Mr. Gyuricza, please let me take the bag."

"Okay."

Tom took it from Dad and said, "I can't believe how heavy this is."

Dad had a look of relief on his face. He said, "I'm glad I don't have to carry it anymore."

We got into the car and drove to our place. On the way, I said, "We're renting a trailer on a nice piece of land. Tom and I love it there."

"Dad and I are looking forward to seeing where you live," Mom replied.

"I think you'll both like it."

As we pulled into the driveway, Mom said, "What a beautiful area. I can understand why you like it here."

"It's very nice," Dad said.

We got out of the car and went inside. Tom took my parents on a tour of the trailer. Afterwards, they sat down and chatted in the living room. Meanwhile, I started heating up the stuffed cabbage and prepared mashed potatoes and green beans. For dessert, I had baked an apple pie the day before.

When the food was ready, we sat down at the table. After Tom and I tasted Mom's stuffed cabbage, I said, "Mom, this is scrumptious."

"Thank you, Yolanda."

"It's delicious," Tom added. "I can't believe you carried this from home into Manhattan on the subway and then brought it on the bus to Vermont."

"I'm happy you're both enjoying it so much," Mom replied.

When I brought dessert to the table, Mom said, "I can't wait to have your homemade apple pie. It looks delicious."

"I hope you and Dad like it."

Mom took one bite and exclaimed, "This pie is wonderful, Yolanda!"

"Yes, it is," said Dad.

"Thank you."

After we finished the meal, Mom and I cleaned up while Tom and my dad sat in the living room and talked. When Mom and I were done, we joined them. Out of the blue, Mom looked at Tom and asked, "Would you please call us 'Mom' and 'Dad' instead of Mr. and Mrs. Gyuricza?"

I could tell Tom was caught off guard by Mom's request. He hesitated a few moments before he answered, "Sure."

We continued to enjoy light conversation for the next hour or so. Before long, we took them back to the bus station and said our goodbyes. They boarded the bus, and as the bus pulled away, we waved to each other.

On the way home, as Tom drove, I snuggled up to him and breathed a sigh of relief. "I'm glad nothing came up about any past conflicts between Mom and me."

"I am too."

"It was nice to see my parents."

"Yes, it was. I enjoyed the time we spent together."

"Me too, Tom. Hopefully, from now on we can have a good relationship with them."

"After how well it went today, I think everything will be okay."

"Tom, you're probably right. I appreciate your optimism."

"I'm sure your parents were relieved to see that we're happily married."

"I agree."

The following week after my parents' visit, a letter came in the mail from Mom. She expressed how much she and Dad enjoyed spending time with us. She also mentioned how sorry she was about the problems she caused in my life before Tom and I got married.

Even though we were still hurting because of everything that had happened in New York leading up to our elopement, we were grateful for what she wrote. However, I knew it would take me time to completely let go of the emotional pain and heartache I had experienced. From that point on, Tom and I wanted to put the past behind us and strive to build a closer relationship with my parents.

In December 1969, we went back to New York for a wedding on my side of the family. After arriving in Queens, we stopped by to see Tom's mom and dropped off our luggage. We planned to stay there while in the area. Next, we visited my parents to spend a short time with them before the wedding that afternoon. Soon after Tom and I got there, I asked Mom, "How are you doing?"

In response, she took me into the bathroom, locked the door, and said, "I want you to see something, Yolanda." She showed me the mastectomy incisions from her operation a year earlier.

I was shocked and said, "Mom, I can't believe your incisions aren't completely healed. Are you having any pain?"

With a tear running down her cheek, she replied, "Sometimes."

"Have you seen the doctor?"

"Yes, he's doing everything he can. I don't want to talk about it anymore, Yolanda."

"Mom, I'm sorry to hear what you're going through since your operation. I'll keep you in my prayers."

"Thank you. Let's go back to the living room and spend time with Dad and Tom."

I felt an ache in my stomach as we left the bathroom. I thought, *I wish Mom weren't still struggling to regain her health.*

At the wedding reception, Mom appeared to be in good spirits. Tom danced with her during one of the songs the band played. Later that evening, Tom said to me, "While I was dancing with your mom, we were having a pleasant conversation. She smiled and appeared happy. Out of the blue, she said, 'Tom, I don't think I'm going to live much longer.' I was completely surprised. I responded, 'You look terrific. You're not going to die.'"

"After your reply, did she say anything more about dying?"

"No, Yolanda, we just continued chatting."

"When we were at Mom and Dad's house today, Mom showed me the incisions from her surgery last year. They're not healed up yet. Maybe that's why she told you what she did."

"You're probably right."

After the wedding, we spent part of the following week visiting with relatives before returning to Vermont. It was great to see everyone.

Tom and I had celebrated our December birthdays in Vermont earlier in the month. We spent our last day in New York with my parents. It was thoughtful of them to surprise us with a birthday cake and gifts. Our time that day was enjoyable and memorable.

As we were getting ready to leave and go home, we could sense Mom was having a very difficult time saying goodbye. It was hard for us to fully appreciate or understand why, but it was evident that she wanted our time together to last longer. We left with the hope that the next time we saw her, she would be feeling better.

Within a few weeks after returning to Vermont, our landlady, Linnie, stopped by and told us she wanted to move back into her trailer. Tom hadn't signed a lease when he rented from her, so we had to start looking for another place to live. Instead of renting, we decided to look into purchasing a mobile home. Not far from Brattleboro, there was a place that sold them in Hinsdale, New Hampshire. We found a new one we liked. It had a kitchen, living room, bathroom, and two bedrooms. We figured it wouldn't take too many years to pay off, since the price was reasonable. Right above the sales lot on a hill overlooking the Connecticut River, there was a mobile home park where we planned to rent a space.

During January 1970, we started making plans for our move from Vermont to New Hampshire. At the end of the month, I got the fantastic news that I was pregnant. Tom and I were ecstatic. I couldn't wait to tell Mom and Dad about the pregnancy. Just before I phoned them, my Aunt Vera called and told me my mom was in the hospital. After finding out, Tom and I planned to visit her.

The following day, February 1st, I got another call from Aunt Vera. I was overcome with grief to find out Mom had died. With tears in my eyes, I went to Tom and said, "Aunt Vera called to tell me Mom died today."

Tom took me in his arms. "I'm sorry to hear your mom passed away."

"It's hard for me to believe she's gone."

"Me too, Yolanda. What she said to me at the wedding about dying was for real." We sat down on the couch.

"Yeah. Little did we realize it at the time. That's why Mom had such a hard time saying good-bye to us. She probably figured she'd never see us again."

"You're right. Now it all makes sense."

"Tom, let's start packing. We'll head for New York tomorrow morning."

"Okay."

As sad as I felt in losing my mother, I was grateful the time spent with her in December had been pleasant and that our relationship had been completely reconciled.

Chapter 14

Tension Mounts

*E*ARLY IN MARCH 1970, we moved to New Hampshire. It was exciting to have our own place, a beautiful, new mobile home. The metal siding was turquoise and trimmed in white along the top and bottom. Each window had black shutters. The inside walls were covered with walnut-colored paneling. The home was practically maintenance free, which appealed to Tom and me.

One of Tom's co-workers, Ralph, used his pickup truck to help us move the few belongings we owned. He and Tom had become good friends after they met at work.

An advantage of the home was that it came furnished. However, we weren't required to take all the furniture. For anything we didn't want, the salesman reduced the price we owed for the home. Prior to moving, we shopped for a better quality kitchen table and chairs, couch, and bed. What fun we had as newlyweds, walking through a local store and picking out furniture for the first time. After a few weeks of living in the new home, it was exciting to purchase our first television, a portable nineteen-inch black-and-white set.

It was a welcome change from the trailer in Vermont to have more space and an extra bedroom. Living in New Hampshire brought Tom closer to his job. We kept our post office box in Vermont, since he drove through Brattleboro daily to and from work. His usual routine was to leave work and pick up the mail before getting home shortly after 5:00 P.M.

Tom and I liked the mobile home park. Our neighbors were pleasant and we enjoyed getting to know them. It was a peaceful place to live.

One day, I waited for Tom to get home from work. He didn't show up at his usual time and hadn't called about coming home later. I thought, *It's six o'clock. He's almost an hour late. I wonder where he is. Maybe while picking up the mail in Brattleboro, he decided to do some shopping.*

By 6:30, I was so concerned about him I became frantic. My stomach felt queasy and I started getting a throbbing headache. *If he was delayed at work for any reason and couldn't leave at 4:30, he'd call and let me know.*

I couldn't stand waiting any longer, so I called the power plant construction site where he worked. A security guard answered. I asked, "Would you please connect me to my husband's extension? His name is Tom Barbagallo."

"I can't put your call through due to an emergency," the guard responded.

I gave the guard my name and phone number and said, "Please tell Tom to call me as soon as possible."

"I'm not sure if I can do that because of what's going on here," he replied.

Before I could say anything more, he hung up. I sat down on the couch and rested my hands on my large, eight-month-pregnant stomach. Tears streamed down my face. *Oh, God. Please be with Tom and protect him.*

I couldn't think straight. A chill went through my body as I imagined what might have happened. *It must be a very serious situation if Tom can't call me. I hope he's okay.*

To make matters worse, about a week earlier Tom had witnessed the aftermath of a fatal accident at work. While outside at the construction site, he had walked around the corner of a building and heard a thunderous explosion that shook the ground. A split second later, he was shocked to see a severely injured worker lying on the ground. Tom and others rushed to the aid of the man, but attempts to help him failed. Sadly, he died en route to the hospital.

Before the tragedy, the man had been assigned to use a handheld torch to cut the tops off empty fifty-five gallon steel drums to make them into trash cans. The flame from his torch ignited fumes coming from a drum of paint thinner, stored horizontally about three car lengths away from him. He was facing the drum when the explosion occurred. The cover blew off and hit him in the face. *I wish Tom hadn't told me the details of the accident. I can't stop thinking about it. What am I going to do if something happened to Tom?*

I looked at the kitchen clock several times while sitting in the living room. Gripping fear overtook me. With the recent fatality at work on my mind and the fact that I still hadn't heard from Tom by 7:45, I broke out in a cold sweat and my heart started to palpitate. *Why isn't he home yet?*

I got up and paced back and forth for a few minutes between the bedroom and kitchen. Next, I sat on the Early American rocking chair in the living room. I rocked back and forth nervously, prayed for Tom's safety, and hoped he was all right.

Desperately needing a diversion, I walked into the bedroom and turned on the TV. I went through the channels and found the Oral Roberts program. It was being televised from Japan. I had never seen his program before, but it looked interesting, so I sat down on the bed and watched it. The beautiful songs and his encouraging message helped to keep my mind somewhat occupied. Toward the end of the show, a free souvenir was offered with an address to request one. It was a plastic, translucent paperweight that contained a white pearl inside a seashell with the inscription, "Christ – The Pearl of Great Price." I planned to mail for it the next day.

I turned the TV off, walked into the kitchen, and heard a key turning in the doorknob. My heart leaped for joy as Tom walked in. I flew into his arms and exclaimed, "I've been worried sick about you! It's after nine o'clock! What happened?"

Tom kissed me tenderly and said, "Let's sit down and I'll tell you."

"I'm relieved to know that you're okay."

"I'm very sorry for getting home this late and not being able to let you know. There was a bomb scare at work just before quitting time.

There are people that don't want the nuclear plant to be completed. They may try anything to stop or delay the project. Due to security concerns, I wasn't permitted to call out, receive calls, or leave work during the crisis."

"That's why I couldn't get through to you, Tom, when I called and spoke with a security guard. I asked him to leave you a message. Did you get it?"

"No."

"Tom, please hold me tight in your arms." As he pulled me close to him, I rested my head on his shoulder and continued, "I never want to go through another evening like this."

"I understand, Yolanda. I don't want you having to deal with this kind of situation in the future without knowing that I'm okay. I'll have to find a way to get a message to you if anything delays me from getting home."

"What would have happened if I had to get to the hospital to have our baby?"

"I'll talk with a few of our neighbors. I'm sure one of them would be willing to take you there if you can't get hold of me."

"That's a good idea."

"How are you feeling, Yolanda?"

"Much better now that you're home, Tom. Did you have any supper?"

"No. How about you?"

"Just a few pretzels. I had no appetite while waiting for you. How about I make us ham sandwiches and then we can go to bed?"

"Sounds good." Tom got up from the couch and took my hands to help me stand up. He spoke softly in my ear, "I love you."

"I love you too, Sweetheart."

While we ate dinner, I told Tom about the Oral Roberts program and the free souvenir that was offered.

The following day, I stayed in bed longer than usual after Tom left for work. *I'm exhausted. My back hurts and I feel drained, physically and emotionally. I'm uncomfortable with this huge stomach. Only one month to go and I'll give birth to our first child. Tom and I will be happy to have either a boy or a girl. It doesn't matter which one, as long as the baby's healthy.*

During my last month of pregnancy, Tom made it a point to call me from work a number of times during the day to see how I was doing. I always looked forward to hearing from him.

One night after supper, I stood at the sink and washed the dishes. Suddenly, I yelled, "Tom, I'm starting to feel contractions. I think we should go to the hospital."

"Get ready to leave, and I'll put your luggage in the car," he replied excitedly.

Off we went to the local hospital in Brattleboro, which was no more than fifteen minutes away. Tom stayed with me at least three hours in the labor room. I appreciated his holding my hand as I continued having contractions. Suddenly, the contractions subsided. A half hour later, a nurse came to check on me. When I told her the contractions had stopped, she looked at Tom and said, "There's no sense in your staying here. You may as well go home and get some sleep. I'm going to move your wife to a hospital room. A nurse will call you when Yolanda goes into the delivery room."

"Okay." He kissed me good night and said, "I love you, Sweetheart. See you soon."

"Good night, Tom. I can't wait to have our baby."

The next morning, October 10, 1970, a nurse called Tom and told him to come to the hospital. Later that morning, I gave birth to a baby girl. We named her Karen. I was thrilled when Tom came into my room. "Look at our gorgeous daughter."

"She's beautiful, Yolanda, just like you!" He kissed me and Karen.

"What do you think of her full head of jet black hair, Tom?"

"It's amazing. I never realized newborn babies could have that much hair."

What a wonderful day. Tom and I became parents for the first time. He left the hospital and returned a short time later with a dozen red roses. With tears of joy, I said, "Thanks for the beautiful roses."

After I got home from the hospital, Tom's mother came by bus from New York and stayed a week to help me with Karen. It was an exciting time, both for me as a new mother and for her as the grandmother of another grandchild.

A week after she left to go back home, my souvenir arrived in the mail. It was more beautiful than I expected. Some time later, we started receiving a monthly magazine called *Abundant Life*. We read it from cover to cover and enjoyed the interesting and uplifting articles. In spite of going through that traumatic evening waiting for Tom, I was grateful that something good had come out of it.

Chapter 15

Curiosity Aroused

❧

TOM AND I were content with our lives. What more could we ask for? I was happy as a stay-at-home mom taking care of Karen, and Tom had a job he enjoyed.

As Roman Catholics, we attended church once a week and on designated holy days. We did our best to follow the teachings of the church and treat others the way we wanted to be treated. That's what we understood about Christianity.

When I was a teenager, my parents had given me a Bible with the Old and New Testaments. I remember holding it in my lap, opening to the first page in Genesis, and reading a few verses. I didn't get any further. Tom had gotten his first New Testament portion of the Bible a few years before we met. He was watching a religious TV program and they offered a free copy that he requested. Like me, he didn't get past the first page. Occasionally, Tom and I talked about reading the Bible for ourselves, but somehow we couldn't get motivated to start.

While living in the rental trailer, we had attended a Catholic church in Putney, Vermont. It was a small country church. When going to Mass on Saturday evenings, there were never more than a dozen people there. What a sharp contrast compared to the hundreds of people that attended the large churches we went to in New York.

At the country church, the priest was cheerful and friendly. He stood just inside the door of the church and greeted everyone as they entered.

One time we were running a little late and arrived after everyone else. As we walked in, the priest was still standing at the door. He looked at us with a big smile and said, "I was sure you were coming, so I waited for you to get here."

"Thank you," we replied. Tom and I smiled. It made us feel good that he delayed starting the Mass until we arrived.

After moving to Hinsdale, New Hampshire, we attended church either there or in Brattleboro, since it took about the same time to get to either church. The Masses we liked most were those where musicians played guitars to lead the congregation in singing. As much as it felt good to be in church every Sunday, we still wanted to learn more about the Bible.

One day, Tom came home from work and out of the blue, he said, "I'm going to begin reading the New Testament I got years ago."

"What made you decide to start?"

"Let's sit down and I'll tell you what happened."

"Okay."

"I met a nice guy recently at work. His name is John and he's around our age. Today we had lunch together. I found out something interesting about him."

"What is it?"

"He reads the Bible."

"Really?"

"Yes. He told me his life has become much more fulfilling since he started reading it."

"What do you mean, Tom?"

"I asked him the same thing. He said that he has more peace of mind, is much happier, and feels closer to God."

"That's amazing."

"It is, Yolanda. I told him I've been thinking about reading the Bible too."

"Are you going to start soon?"

"Tomorrow."

"When will you find time?"

"At work during lunch break."

"Maybe sometime I'll get into reading it too."

When Tom and I dated and early in our marriage, I had never heard him use foul language. After he had been working at the nuclear construction site a few months, he began to change. Many of his co-workers cursed, which rubbed off on him. At times, he used inappropriate language while with me at home and when driving the car. Unfortunately, he influenced me. I started using the same language, which I had never done before.

As Tom read the Bible regularly, I noticed he gradually stopped using foul language. The difference I saw in him affected me in a positive way. My language changed for the better. There were other changes I observed. Tom was more patient when we had occasional disagreements. I also felt he was more sensitive when I shared my feelings with him. He preferred to spend extra time with Karen and me rather than watching TV. The changes in Tom encouraged me.

Sometime later, Tom came across an advertisement in a magazine. It promoted making extra money part-time by selling Bible-based, Christian teachings and songs presented on long- playing stereo records. It seemed like a good opportunity and the start-up cost was reasonable. Tom called the phone number in the ad, spoke with someone about what they had to offer, and explained everything to me. I thought it sounded good. He called back and ordered the sales kit.

There were two sets of records. One, *The Journey to Bethany,* contained a dramatic, six-hour depiction of the life of Christ. The voice on the recordings was depicted as that of the Lord speaking word for word from the Scriptures to portray His teachings. The other series of records, *The Library of Life,* was primarily for teens. It presented Christian values along with lively spiritual songs for young people.

Tom memorized a lengthy sales presentation and listened to the records many times to become knowledgeable about the teachings and songs. Sometimes I listened along with him.

As it turned out, Tom didn't pursue this venture for long. However, it was a great investment because it helped us become more familiar with the Bible.

Chapter 16

On the Move

ᴵN EARLY MAY 1971, Tom came home from work one day and said, "I found out my assignment at the plant could end within four to six months."

"I can't believe it. I thought you'd be there at least another year."

"Me too. I was told there's a chance my job could get extended, but it's not a sure thing."

All Tom knew at the time was that his New York City-based company ultimately had plans to transfer him back to Manhattan or to a nuclear construction site in another state. We loved living in New Hampshire and being close to Vermont. As much as we missed our relatives in New York and would have liked to be near them, Tom didn't want to work in Manhattan again. After experiencing rural living for almost two years, we didn't find the idea of going back to the city appealing.

Tom felt compelled to search for another job because his future was uncertain. Within a month, he had an interview scheduled with an engineering firm in Reading, Pennsylvania. I rode along with him as he drove there. Close friends babysat Karen.

That afternoon, we arrived at the motel where the company had made arrangements for us to stay. After an early dinner, we drove around the area beyond the outskirts of Reading. What a delight to see similarities to Vermont and New Hampshire.

I said, "Look at the beautiful scenery." I pointed out my window and continued excitedly, "Do you see the horses and cows grazing in the meadows?"

"Yes, Yolanda. It's like back home."

"It is. This area would be a wonderful place to live."

"You're right."

The next day, Tom had the interview while I waited at the motel. Later that afternoon, he returned and said, "Yolanda, my interview went well. I think they want to hire me. It's an engineering position in the home office here in Reading. Eventually, I'll have to travel on occasion, but it shouldn't be longer than a few days at a time."

"Sounds great! I hope you get the job."

"Me too."

That evening, Tom received a call at the motel from the manager who had interviewed him. After getting off the phone he smiled and yelled, "I got the job!"

I flew into his strong arms and gave him a giant bear hug. I kissed him and exclaimed, "Congratulations! That's fantastic!"

In August 1971, we moved to Pennsylvania and Tom started his new job. Karen was ten months old. We stayed at the same motel where we had been during his interview. This time, we were there two weeks while waiting for our mobile home to arrive. It was moved at the company's expense from New Hampshire to a mobile home park near Birdsboro, Pennsylvania.

Shortly after moving, we found a Catholic church to attend in Birdsboro. One Sunday morning before church, Tom turned on the television in the bedroom while he waited for me to get ready. I was combing my hair in the bathroom when he yelled, "Yolanda, please come here and look at this program. There's a minister on from Akron, Ohio. His name is Rex Humbard."

"Okay, I'm coming." I stood inside the bedroom door to watch and listen to what he had to say. Within ten minutes the program was over.

"I liked his sermon," Tom said.

"Me too."

"Let's watch him next week, Yolanda."

"All right."

The following Sunday we saw the program. We continued to watch it weekly before church. Rex Humbard made the Bible come alive when he spoke about the Lord and His teachings. His sermons were thought provoking and inspiring.

After watching the program for at least a month, it was obvious we were starting to connect with what he was sharing. Tom said, "Since we've been watching Rex, I've had a desire to have a deeper relationship with God."

"I feel the same, Tom."

At the end of each sermon Rex brought up the same two points for consideration to his church congregation and television audience. The first was typically stated, "If you are sure you would go to heaven if you died right now, raise your hand." It was amazing to see most of the people raise their hands. We wondered how they could be certain about going to heaven.

As far as we were concerned, our final destination after dying was unclear. It was always a hope that we would eventually get to heaven, but not until we spent time in another place to suffer for our sins. It was our belief that we were not worthy or good enough to go directly to heaven. The only other option that we knew about was hell, and we certainly didn't want to go there. What we understood about hell was that it was a place of torment lasting forever.

The second point he presented was, "If you don't know you are going to heaven when you die but would like to know for sure, raise your hand." He invited those who were uncertain to say a prayer of repentance and make a decision to accept Jesus Christ as their personal Savior. Every Sunday, we observed people at the church raising their hands and saying a prayer that Rex asked them to repeat after him.

In watching the program every week, we came to the realization that what he did to lead people to pray and be sure of going to heaven was based on what the Bible teaches. We began to understand why he presented the two points to people regarding their final destination after dying. While watching the program on a Sunday morning in October 1971, we decided to pray with Rex so we could be certain about going to heaven.

Tom and I felt different after saying the prayer, as simple as it was. Neither of us had ever prayed like that in the past. We were both sitting on the bed. Tom looked at me affectionately. With eyes sparkling, he said, "I feel like a weight has come off me. I can't remember feeling such peace and contentment."

"I feel the same way. What happened to us?"

"I don't exactly know, Yolanda, but I'm sure it's the start of a good thing."

"You're right. And you know what?"

"Tell me."

"For the first time in my life, Tom, I'm determined to start reading the Bible."

"That's great. I want to get into it much more than in the past. Why don't we read it together some evenings after Karen goes to bed?"

"Sounds good to me, Tom."

I began reading the New Testament, and Tom and I read parts of it together. Within a few weeks, we wanted to study the Scriptures in more depth with other people who had the same interest.

At the time, there weren't any Bible studies at the church we attended. I checked the Yellow Pages of the phone book and called several local Bible churches in our area. One of them had a Bible study every Friday night with child care provided. When we went for the first time, the pastor, his wife, and many others greeted Tom and me. They had a time of prayer and Bible study and everyone made us feel welcome. After the first visit, we decided to go back, since it was exciting to learn more about the Scriptures and to interact with the friendly people at the church. Karen enjoyed playing with other children in the nursery.

We continued going to the Catholic church on Sundays while attending the Friday night Bible study. One Saturday morning, Tom asked, "How would you like to visit the Bible church tomorrow?"

"That's a great idea."

"I'd like to see what it's like, Yolanda."

"Me too."

On Sunday morning, as Tom, Karen, and I went into the church, we were greeted enthusiastically by the pastor and others we knew from Friday nights. After dropping Karen off at the nursery, we found a seat near the back of the church. We enjoyed the pastor's sermon and the service. The following week we went back, and afterwards continued to attend on Sundays. It was a pleasure socializing with people after the service.

Some may wonder why we left the Catholic church. We really had no plans to go elsewhere. As we were seeking God's direction, it became apparent that the change in churches was part of His will for our lives. However, we have no intention of telling anyone which church to attend, because it's a personal matter between each individual and God.

After we prayed with Rex Humbard, our main focus began to center on following the Scriptures as a pattern for our daily lives.

One day, Tom mentioned something he remembered from when he was about eleven years old. He and his mom were having lunch with his cousins, Angie and Joe from New York. Before the meal, Angie said a beautiful prayer in her own words that was meaningful to him. It was the first time he had ever heard anyone pray like that at the table. Also, he recalled that these cousins were loving and kind in a way that made a positive impression on him. Tom's father had died when he was four years old, and these relatives were on his dad's side of the family, so the visits were occasional.

After sharing this memory with me, he said, "I think my cousins might have had a spiritual experience similar to ours."

"Really?"

"Yes, Yolanda. I think we should send them a letter and share what recently happened to us."

"I agree."

"Would you be willing to write it?"

"Sure, I'd be glad to."

Soon after mailing the letter, we received a great response. The following is an excerpt:

Dearest Cousins Tom, Yolanda, and Karen,

Many thanks from our hearts for the delightful, joyous letter sent to us! I (Angie) didn't even wait to get inside the door to read it, but read it near the mailbox, and the tears just fell, and right there my heart was so full of praise to God. Our dear cousins have accepted Christ Jesus into their hearts!

Joe and I, since children, have been born again, and have tried to make Him Lord of our lives.

Many thanks for your compliments as we in turn give all the glory and praise to God, if in a small measure, we have somehow been of influence to Tom. We attend the First Presbyterian Church in Flushing at present and enjoy attending a Baptist Church also. We are of Pentecostal background. My father at 81 years of age is still preaching the old fashioned gospel. Praise God!

What a lovely name, our cousin's name is, Karen. She must be a delight to you. How wonderful, dear cousins Tom and Yolanda, to be able to raise your daughter in the nurture and admonition of the Lord and attend church together.

How many years we have prayed, feeling the burden for our families, relatives, and friends.

Ours is to sow the seed, be of example, emulating Christ Jesus and refining our relationship with our Lord and with man daily. God will water and give the increase. There is none other name under heaven, given among men whereby we must be saved.

Thank God that He can satisfy the hungry heart and the soul searching after Him for a greater walk with God.

Love from us all to you,

Angie and Joe

Chapter 17

Wide Open Spaces

ℰ

IN NOVEMBER 1972, I got pregnant with our second child. Now that our family was going to expand, we needed a larger place to live. Tom and I had the dream to buy or build a home in the country.

A friend and co-worker, Norm, and his wife, Donna, invited us to attend a Bible study at their home. It was located in a lovely wooded area. We enjoyed the evening with them and their friends.

Tom and I liked the neighborhood where they lived. About a month later, Tom found out from Norm that there might be land available down the road from him where we could have a house built. To our delight, after Tom checked with the people who owned the land, they were willing to sell it to us.

In the spring of 1973, we bought one and a half acres of wooded land in Lancaster County, Pennsylvania. How exciting to anticipate living in a country setting surrounded by Amish and Mennonite farms. The builder, Irvin, had built a number of homes up the road from our property. He lived in one of them, making it convenient to deal with him.

Tom and I chose a three bedroom, bi-level style home from a picture we saw in a house plan magazine. Rather than order the blueprint, Tom got ideas from the picture and drew up a detailed sketch with dimensions. He showed it to Irvin, who felt it had enough detail that a blueprint wasn't necessary.

The arrangement for building our home was on a time and materials basis, which meant that any work Tom did would save money. Therefore, he spent long hours after his regular job and on Saturdays at the construction site. Irvin left specific things for him to do, such as roofing, nailing floors, and installing insulation. He took vacation time off from his job to assist in framing the house.

One morning after the framing had begun, a worker, John, arrived later than everyone else. He was greeted by two men as "Pappy." Tom started addressing him the same way, since he thought it was a nickname. At a later date, when the house was almost completed, Tom found out the two men referring to John as "Pappy" were his sons. Tom apologized to John who just laughed and said, "That's okay."

During the early construction stage after the framing was done and the house was under roof, Tom's mother and brother Vin visited for a weekend. The main purpose of the trip was to work Saturday and add extra wood bracing throughout the structure. Vin had valuable experience in home construction. He knew what could be done to make the house much sturdier.

That evening, Mom and I found out how the day had gone. Vin said, "We got on the roof because I wanted to show Tom something. As we stood on the top center portion of the roof, I asked Tom to sway his body from side to side. I did the same thing."

"I couldn't believe it, Yolanda. The frame and roof moved back and forth!" Tom exclaimed.

"I told Tom that when the bracing is added, we'd get on the roof again to check it out," Vin said.

He started under the roof and worked down through the structure. Tom assisted him and the work was completed by late afternoon. Vin said, "When we got back on the roof and tried to make the structure sway from side to side, it didn't move."

"I was amazed to see all the extra bracing Vin added," Tom said. "It definitely made a tremendous difference."

"Thanks very much, Vin, for all you did to improve the integrity of our home," I said.

One Saturday, Tom worked long hours installing insulation. He didn't bring food along and got hungry but didn't want to take time to go eat out. Instead he drove a few minutes to a bake shop in a nearby Amish home. A freshly baked pumpkin pie caught his eye. After returning to the house, he ate the whole pie. He was no longer hungry but didn't want pumpkin pie again for a long time!

During that summer while Tom worked on our future home, I was pregnant and couldn't wait until the baby arrived. Finally, the day came when I gave birth to our second gorgeous daughter, Michele. Unlike Karen's full head of black hair, hers was blonde peach fuzz.

In the mobile home park where we lived, our friendly neighbor, Pat, gave us a beautiful redwood wall hanging. She had had it custom made. It was decorated with two ceramic birds, one white and the other pink. Carved into the wood are the words, "IT'S A GIRL! MICHELE LYNN BARBAGALLO. AUG 16, 1973 – 12:26 PM, WT. 7 LBS. 12 OZ. LENGTH 20 ½"

After our home was built but not completely finished inside, we were glad to move in a few weeks before Christmas, December 1973. Our daughters, Karen and Michele, were three years old and four months old. We enjoyed being nestled in the woods surrounding our home. Tom kept busy painting ceilings and walls and staining doors and trim.

We weren't familiar with the Amish and Mennonites until we moved to Lancaster County. They are industrious, hardworking, and friendly people. Some don't drive cars but use horse-drawn buggies for transportation. It was a treat for us and our relatives to see buggies pass our home. We still enjoy watching them go by!

One of our neighbors, a Mennonite family, lived on a nearby dairy farm. The couple had ten children and they used a horse and buggy for transportation. Their older daughters babysat Karen and Michele. They seemed to enjoy watching TV when they came over, since their family didn't have one. Typically, families like this don't have a TV. After returning home one night, I asked our babysitter, Lucy, "Do you miss having a TV at home?"

"No," she replied.

Her reply was humorous because whenever we got home, the TV would usually be on with the volume turned up high.

Until we moved to Lancaster County, we had never heard of phone service with a party line. What a drastic change from having a private line. There were no other options for our location, since we were at the end of our local telephone company's service area. It took seven years before we could get a private line. When we entertained relatives or friends, they wondered why we didn't pick up the phone when it rang. We told them only a party line was available and that each of the five families on the same line had a different-sounding ring. Therefore, we only picked up the phone when we heard our ring.

A big disadvantage was that it wasn't always possible to make a call. On numerous occasions, when we picked up the phone to use it, there were people having lengthy conversations. It was inconvenient to keep picking up the phone to check whether the line was free.

Tom told one of his co-workers, Paul, about the party line. He laughed and asked, "Does your phone need to be cranked like in the old days?"

One evening, Tom and I had to go out unexpectedly and needed a babysitter. I picked up the phone to call our neighbor and recognized her voice on the party line as she talked with a lady. I said, "Sorry for interrupting, Mrs. Horst. This is Yolanda. I need one of your girls to babysit right away."

"Laura is available. Can you come and fetch her?" she replied.

"Sure. Thank you, Mrs. Horst."

As a part of living in the country, animals and reptiles are in close proximity to our home. It's fascinating to see deer and an occasional fox while looking out the window. At times, box turtles have shown up on our lawn and in the woods. One summer in the middle of the night, Tom awakened to loud snoring. As he listened carefully, he realized it wasn't me because the noise was coming from outside. He jumped out of bed, went to the open window, and was in for a big surprise. A huge buck (male deer with antlers) was standing in our driveway, snorting!

Garter snakes are plentiful where we live. We've seen them in the most unlikely places, for instance, sunning themselves on the wood pile in front of the house and living in the old redwood shed adjacent to our driveway. Tom stored firewood inside the shed along with our bikes. Whenever we went to get the bikes, there were at least six to eight snakes lying in and on top of the woodpile. Tom told the girls and me, "Ignore the snakes. They're afraid of you and will hide if they feel threatened."

Usually we walked in and out and the snakes stayed where they were. One Saturday morning, I went into the shed to get my bike, and one of the snakes was apparently startled and fell off the woodpile onto my sneakers. I jumped back, let out a deafening scream, and dashed out of the shed without my bike. Tom came running from inside the house and asked, "What happened?"

"I'll never go back in the shed until you get rid of all the snakes!"

"I'll have to remove the wood we're storing in there and the snakes at the same time," Tom replied.

"How soon can you do it?"

"Right away, Yolanda."

He started removing the wood while wearing heavy-duty gloves to protect his hands from the snakes. It was easier said than done. He had to capture each snake by using a stick to hold the head down while grabbing the snake behind the head. After he caught each one, he brought it across the road from our house and threw it into the woods. He removed the wood and at least sixteen snakes.

Tom was convinced he had taken care of the problem and we had seen the last of the snakes. A few days later, he walked into the shed and a snake was hanging just inside the doorway at Tom's eye level. He got scared and quickly backed out of the shed. The snake fell to the floor and slithered away. Except for an occasional snake, the shed was safe enough for the girls and me to get our bikes. What a relief! Eventually, we replaced this thirty-year-old shed. We donated it to a neighboring farmer who planned to use it as a chicken coop.

A few years before we gave away the redwood shed, Lee, our kind and helpful neighbor, moved it with Tom to another location on our property. It was time to purchase a much larger one. The rear portion of the driveway where the old shed had been standing would have to be extended considerably before being paved. Many truckloads of crushed stone were needed to fill up the area that would become home for the new twelve-by-sixteen-foot red barn shed that Tom had ordered from a local shed dealer.

In the planning stage, Tom's brother Joe visited to help plan the driveway extension. They took measurements and staked out the area. After the driveway addition was completed and the shed arrived, Joe visited and liked how everything looked. Tom wanted to include lights and electric outlets in the shed. Joe suggested adding insulation, finishing the interior ceiling and walls, and adding baseboard heating for the cold weather. Tom agreed. Joe explained how to do it, since he had worked as a full-time carpenter contractor.

As the months passed, along with Joe's periodic visits and help, the work progressed. They used rough-sawn wood paneling and pine boards to finish the interior.

When Joe came to see the completed project, he said, "The ceiling and walls look great with a natural finish. I suggest that you cover the plywood floor with vinyl or carpeting."

"That sounds like a good idea," Tom replied.

After thinking about it, Tom and I decided to have a light blue carpet installed. Of course, Joe came to see it. When Tom opened the double doors, Joe stepped inside and said, "It's very nice. The carpeting looks great."

"If Tom gets out of hand, he'll have to sleep in the shed," I said jokingly.

Joe laughed and replied, "That might not be bad, since it's like a studio apartment."

We'll always be grateful for Joe's involvement in the shed project from start to finish.

When the grandparents were alive, we enjoyed celebrating our children's birthdays with them. Tom's mom and stepdad would visit for Karen's in October, and my dad came for Michele's in August.

During one of the weekend visits for Karen's birthday, it was a warm evening and the windows were open with the attic fan running to cool down the house. Tom brought up the topic of skunks. He said, "We used to leave cat food in a dish outside the front door for our cat, Smokey, since he spends most of his time outdoors. A skunk came by regularly to eat it. After almost getting sprayed by the skunk while going out the door, we decided not to leave cat food outside anymore."

"I never smelled a skunk before," Tom's mom said. "What's it like?"

"I can't describe it, Mom. It's disgusting."

A few seconds later, a skunk sprayed outside the house. The attic fan quickly drew the odor inside. Tom and I rushed to shut off the attic fan and close the windows.

"What's that horrible smell?" Mom asked.

"That's a skunk that just sprayed," Tom replied. "Now you know how bad they smell."

My dad usually visited for a few weeks. He encouraged us to go out on dates, since he was available to babysit. This allowed him to spend quality time alone with his granddaughters, playing games such as monopoly and hide and seek. When we went out during the week, we couldn't stay out late, since Tom had to get up early for work the next day. When we arrived home, it was amusing because Dad always said the same thing, "You're back so early!"

"Dad, we can't stay out too late because Tom has to work tomorrow," I'd usually reply.

It seemed that he wanted us to come back later so he could have more time playing with the girls without us around. He probably would have been delighted if we had gone out every night during his visits.

One day as I read a local newspaper, I came across an ad for volunteers to help with a therapeutic horseback riding program for people dealing with mental/physical disabilities. I was interested and showed Tom the ad. The idea of working with horses and people with special needs appealed to us. We attended an informational meeting at the huge barn where the program would take place and signed up as volunteers on a once-a-week basis during that summer. There was no formalized training. The program coordinator, Mary, patiently helped us greenhorns learn the ropes.

Jack, a good-natured horse, was assigned to us. We had to prepare him in his stall for riding. This involved grooming his brown coat with various brushes for different parts of his body and cleaning hoofs by bending each knee and holding his leg up while scraping the underside of the hoofs clean. Next, we put on the halter, a rope with a headstall for leading a horse. After that, we put on a blanket and saddle and then the bridle, which includes a headstall, bit, and reins. After completion of this phase, Tom led Jack to the barn's open area where our twenty-three-year-old female rider, Susan, waited to mount up. She was assigned to us for each weekly session. We developed a bond with her from the start.

By using a ramp and platform, riders were able to climb on a horse with assistance from an instructor. Meanwhile, the leader kept the horse stationary and the side walker helped the rider get safely situated into the saddle and stirrups.

Tom stood in front of Jack to lead him while I walked alongside with one hand on Susan's leg to help her remain safely mounted and secure. Our instructor, Helen, an experienced rider, was always within a distance where she could verbally communicate instructions to Tom.

There were routines where Tom led Jack around cones in various directions and in circles around the inside perimeter of the barn. In addition, Susan participated in games while mounted on Jack with him standing still, one of which was throwing a large ball into a hoop. Whenever she scored, it was a delight to see the happy look on her face. Even though she wasn't able to speak, she expressed her joy with giggles and big smiles as she was riding and playing the games.

Sometimes we went outdoors and followed a bridle path. Helen walked with us and had Tom lead Jack away from the barn through a shady scenic area with tall trees on both sides of the path. After we got to a designated spot, we headed back to the barn.

Despite temperatures in the nineties and oppressive humidity during the sessions, we remained highly motivated and enthusiastic. It was a great opportunity to help with the summer horseback riding program. Tom and I loved working together as a team. It's one of our favorite memories.

Over the years we've lived in Lancaster County, it has always been enjoyable spending quality time with relatives and friends. Out-of-town guests have been introduced to Pennsylvania Dutch dishes that were new to them, such as three-bean salad, seven layered salad, and shoo-fly pie.

Three-bean salad is a combination of kidney beans, green beans, and yellow wax beans. This mixture is marinated overnight with diced onions, oil, and vinegar. Seven layered salad includes lettuce, green peas, sliced hard-boiled eggs, bacon, and onions covered with mayonnaise and topped with shredded cheddar cheese. Shoo-fly pie consists of molasses, brown sugar, and flour. This pie originally got its name when it was baked and put on the window sill to cool down. The sweet aroma attracted flies and they had to be shooed away.

Another special treat are the cinnamon twist buns freshly made at a nearby Amish bakeshop. One of the reasons they taste scrumptious is because they're deep fried in lard (pig fat). To this day, our nephew Vinny is crazy about them. Whenever he visits, he can't stop eating the cinnamon buns.

It's always a pleasure to take guests to see popular local attractions, such as the Strasburg Rail Road, Kitchen Kettle Village, Sight and Sound Theater, and pretzel factories.

In Strasburg, a coal-burning locomotive with passenger cars travels to Paradise, Pennsylvania, and returns to the station. During the forty-five minute ride, passengers enjoy the scenic countryside with its Amish and Mennonite farms. This is definitely an exciting experience for people of all ages.

At Kitchen Kettle, there are over thirty interesting shops. It's fun strolling through the village and sampling the delicious jams, jellies, and relishes. The luscious aroma from the on-site bakery permeates the village. Watching fudge being made in a huge copper kettle and tasting samples attract people.

Theater performances at Sight and Sound bring Bible stories to life on one of the world's largest stages. The dynamic cast, live animals, and elaborate sets create an atmosphere for productions that are awesome and inspiring.

It's fascinating to watch hard pretzels being made, and the aroma while they're baking is mouth-watering. What a treat to taste a warm, freshly made pretzel right out of the oven! Most companies make them in large quantities on a mass production basis. At one place, there are Amish and Mennonite ladies rolling and twisting pretzels by hand. Anyone interested in seeing an online tour of their facility can go to www.martinspretzels.pa.com.

After experiencing country living in Pennsylvania since 1974, it seems like we've always lived here. It's quite a contrast from where we were born and raised, and yet those days of city living are precious to us. We have wonderful memories of growing up in our families, meeting each other, and falling in love. The hustle and bustle of city living was a normal part of our lives. We never had any intention to move away from New York. Little did we know that God had other plans for us.

Chapter 18

Expanding Horizons

$\mathcal{W}$ HEN OUR DAUGHTERS, Karen and Michele, were young, I thoroughly enjoyed doing fun and interesting things with them.

I purchased a craft book for young children. The girls liked doing activities such as finger painting, toothpick and button art, and making puppets from brown paper bags. Another craft was forming salt and flour dough into various shapes such as smiley faces and hearts that we baked, cooled down, and painted.

One supervised activity they loved was crayon melts. The procedure was to remove the paper from the crayons, cover a griddle with a sheet of heavy duty aluminum foil, and preheat it. Next, I laid two sheets of white paper next to each other on top of the heated foil. The crayons melted as the girls drew pictures and designs on the surface of the heated paper. When the paper was removed from the griddle, the crayon melts solidified and were ready to be displayed on the refrigerator.

As they got older, the girls helped me in the kitchen, making stuffed pizza, other meals, cookies, and desserts. They gladly did chores such as washing and drying dishes, dusting furniture, and cleaning the bathroom sink. I appreciated their pitching in with the housework. These early years with my children will always have a special place in my heart.

After Karen and Michele grew up and moved away from home, Tom and I were on our own again like when we first got married. It was hard to believe how quickly the girls' childhoods and teen years flew by. Here we were in the empty nest stage of our lives.

I missed the years when our daughters were at home because of all that we did together when they were younger.

One day, Tom and I were browsing in a hardware store and unexpectedly met a friend, Suzanne. We hadn't seen her for a while. As we caught up on what was happening in our lives, she said, "Larry and I are full-time foster parents for a seven-year-old girl."

"That sounds interesting. How's it working out?" I asked.

"We love it. I think you and Tom would make great foster parents. You should consider it."

We learned that she and Larry were connected with The Bair Foundation, which offered the option of full-time or respite foster care.

"What's respite care?" I asked.

Suzanne explained, "It involves relieving full-time foster parents on weekends, from Friday night until late Sunday afternoon. Let me give you an 800 number and you can call for an information packet."

"Thanks a lot," I responded.

We said good-bye to each other. On the way home in the car, Tom and I decided to check into the possibility of doing foster care. I called The Bair Foundation and requested information. When it arrived, we looked it over and felt that respite care would be the best option for us. We had extensive paperwork to complete, and a criminal history and child abuse check had to be conducted by the state.

A foundation representative, Marilyn, came to our home and interviewed us as a couple and individually using a lengthy checklist. She asked personal questions relating to many areas of our lives, including our relationship as husband and wife. Marilyn inquired, "Do you have any preference regarding the race of children you take into your home?"

"No," Tom and I replied in unison.

"What do you expect to achieve with the children?" she asked.

"We want them to enjoy their time with us," I said.

"And we want to do everything possible to make them feel welcome in our home," Tom added.

After the interview, Marilyn said, "You'll be required to attend an indoctrination meeting as well as ongoing training sessions, workshops, and seminars.

"I can't wait until we get started," I said enthusiastically.

"Me too," said Tom.

Marilyn said, "As a convenience, The Bair Foundation uses hired drivers to transport the children to and from foster homes. This is an advantage, since quite a few of the children will be coming a long distance to your home."

During the two years Tom and I did foster care, we enjoyed having twenty different children in our home, some of whom we had multiple times. The names of the children we share about have been changed to protect their privacy.

Many of the younger children called us "Mommy" and "Daddy." Our weekends with them were busy, and the time went by quickly. We took long walks, talked non-stop, and played games such as hide and seek, tag, baseball, and badminton. Watching videos was enjoyable and relaxing after spending endless hours outdoors.

It was exciting to get our first phone call to take care of a fourteen-year-old girl. We looked forward to her visit with much anticipation. I was delighted to put her name, Samantha, on my calendar for the Friday we expected her.

When the day arrived and she got to our home, we welcomed her, sat down in the living room, and chatted awhile. Afterwards, Tom suggested we go to a flea market, which definitely appealed to us ladies. It was fun browsing. Samantha's eyes lit up when she saw bright green earrings and a matching necklace. She held them in her hands and exclaimed, "These are beautiful, aren't they?"

"Yes, they are," I replied.

Tom and I decided to purchase the items for her. She was thrilled. With a big smile, she said, "I love them. Thanks very much."

After we returned home and had dinner, Tom asked, "How would you like some popcorn?"

"Sounds great," I said.

"Sure. I love popcorn," Samantha added.

After Tom made it in the microwave and burned it, she started laughing hysterically. He asked her, "What's so funny?"

"My foster dad burns the popcorn just like you," she replied.

Tom made another batch and it was perfect. We enjoyed having Samantha that weekend.

One child we had came from the home of our friend, Suzanne, who had recommended that Tom and I get involved in foster care. It was fun having her seven-year-old foster child, Sally. She was well-behaved and friendly. We got along great. Two of her favorite activities were watching videos and playing hide and seek outdoors. When we gave Sally a beige teddy bear, she jumped up and down and squealed, "I love it! Thank you!"

One of the snacks we served was rice cakes, and she humorously referred to them as plastic cakes. Whenever Sally wanted more she asked with a big smile, "May I please have another plastic cake?" That seemed to be her favorite snack while she stayed with us.

It was a pleasure to take care of two delightful sisters, Kesia and Kiah, eight and five years old. We had a wonderful experience with them at church on Sunday. During the service we stood to sing worship songs. The girls were too short to see anything. Tom let them stand on the church pew in between him and me. While we were singing, we all stood with our arms wrapped around each other. It felt like we had known these precious girls a long time.

After getting home from church, we sat down at the table to have lunch. Before finishing the meal, Kesia looked at Tom and me and smiled. She politely asked, "Can Kiah and I live with you all the time?"

We were caught by surprise and deeply touched. With a tear in my eye, I responded, "We would love to have you stay here, but it's not possible since you both have full-time foster parents. Tom and I are doing foster care only on weekends."

"I understand," Kesia replied.

We took the girls for a walk and got back in time for the driver to pick them up. When he arrived, Tom and I hugged Kesia and Kiah before they got into the car. Each of us smiled and waved goodbye.

Standing in the driveway, I turned to look at Tom and said, "What a blessing that we bonded with the girls in such a short time."

"Yes, we did."

"I hope we have them again, Tom."

"Me too."

One Friday afternoon, a two-year-old boy, Jamal, was dropped off. The driver brought a playpen for him to sleep in. Jamal looked adorable with his crew cut. After the driver left, I took him for a walk around our property. I thought, *Jamal seems like a nice, quiet little boy. I think I'll be able to manage without Tom here tonight.*

Normally, Tom got home around 5:00 P.M. after finishing his school bus run (Tom started driving a school bus a few years after he left the nuclear power industry). That night was different. After his regular run, he drove students to a sports event. I didn't know when he'd get home.

Soon after I fed Jamal supper, I found him to be challenging. He was extremely hyperactive and couldn't sit still. All he did was run around the house non-stop. I tried to keep him occupied with a cartoon video, but he wasn't interested. There were toys for him to play with, but he didn't want anything to do with them. The only thing that calmed him down was when I held him gently in my arms and rocked him. After doing this for quite awhile, I finally got him to fall asleep.

Close to midnight, Tom arrived home and I was still awake. I said, "Jamal is a handful. I had a difficult evening with him. I'm exhausted."

"I'm sorry I wasn't here to help you, Yolanda. I didn't think I'd get home this late. You can stay in bed in the morning. I'll get up and take care of Jamal."

"Thanks. I'm glad you're finally home."

Early the next day, Tom woke up tired but did his best to take care of Jamal. After giving him breakfast, he took him on a long walk using an umbrella stroller. They stopped in a grassy field and ran around together. When they got back home, Jamal was calmer. Tom took a nap to recover from the previous day's work schedule. Now that I was well rested, I gave Jamal lunch and took him for another walk. As we passed a few nearby farms, Jamal started pointing and laughing when he saw horses and cows. This was a big treat for him, because he was from the city of Harrisburg, Pennsylvania. Whenever he was in the stroller he wanted to take the fluffy white teddy bear we had given him.

After Jamal and I got back home from the walk, Tom was up from his nap and felt better. We decided it was now Jamal's turn to take a nap since he was tired. When Tom put him in the playpen he screamed and climbed out. Tom put him back in the playpen and tried to gently reason with him but that didn't work, so he spoke firmly and Jamal lay down and fell asleep. He woke up three hours later, cheerful and refreshed. We went outside and watched him have fun on a rocking horse we had recently bought for younger foster children.

After we ate supper and spent time playing outdoors again, it was getting close to Jamal's bedtime. We went inside and Tom mentioned it was time for him to go to bed. He started to cry and ran away to another room. Tom took him to the playpen and again firmly spoke to him. In a short time he fell asleep. Jamal slept from 8:00 P.M. Saturday evening all the way through until 8:00 A.M. Sunday morning. He woke up alert, smiling, and happier than the day before.

We enjoyed breakfast and left for church. We sat in one of the pews near the back. During the service a short drama was scheduled and Tom was part of it. When he was on stage waiting to say his lines, I whispered in Jamal's ear, "Look up front."

Everyone was watching the performance quietly and intently. As Jamal stood on the seat beside me, Tom spoke out his lines. Suddenly, Jamal pointed his finger at Tom and yelled, "Daddy!" The people around us turned and looked at him and me and chuckled. When Tom got back to his seat I told him what happened. He smiled and gave Jamal a hug.

The rest of the day was relaxing. Jamal was much more responsive and obedient compared to when he first arrived. When the driver came to pick him up, he cried. Just before he left we gave him extra hugs and also pretzels and cookies to take along. Before they left he calmed down, which made us feel better. It was a privilege to spend the weekend with this dear child.

One weekend, we took care of two girls from different foster homes. Sarah and Rebecca were four and six years old. That Saturday afternoon, I unexpectedly had to work at my sales job in a department store. It was a blessing that our daughter, Michele, was visiting because she helped Tom take care of them.

They took the girls to a petting zoo set up in the parking lot of a nearby country store. When I got home from work, the girls were excited to see me. Rebecca smiled and shouted, "Sarah and I had fun at the petting zoo. I fed a llama!"

"I fed the goats!" Sarah yelled.

"We went on a pony ride too!" Rebecca continued.

"Sarah and Rebecca smiled and giggled the whole time they were on the pony ride," Michele said.

One morning, a secretary from The Bair Foundation called with a special request to take care of a three-year-old boy for a week. I told her I'd talk with Tom and call back. We decided if I could get off from work we'd do it. I got approval from my supervisor.

Carlos was a cute little boy with beautiful black, curly hair. His two favorite expressions were "Watch a movie" and "I'm hungry." He mentioned he liked french fries from McDonald's. After Tom heard this, he got a great idea. While Carlos watched a video in the living room, Tom decided to make fries but not the deep-fried type. After cutting up potatoes and shaping them to look like french fries, he pan fried them with olive oil until they were golden brown. Then Tom called from the kitchen, "Carlos, come here. I have a surprise for you."

When Carlos saw the fries with ketchup on them, his brown eyes bulged with excitement. He couldn't wait to climb onto his chair and sit at the table. After tasting the first fry, he smiled and said, "Yummy," and quickly gobbled up the rest of them. He jumped out of his chair and ran to give Tom a hug.

Since he enjoyed eating, it was always a joy sitting down at the table together. During one of our meals, Carlos jumped out of his chair and came over to where I was seated. He stood beside me with his hands raised, and I picked him up. He gave me a big kiss on the cheek, got down, and did likewise with Tom. Then he ran back to his seat and continued eating.

On a number of occasions while we were walking and holding hands, he would look at me and smile, lift up my hand, and kiss it several times. It was apparent Carlos was a very affectionate child. We were glad to see how happy and comfortable he was with us.

It was late August when we had this child, and Tom's school bus was in our driveway in preparation for the new school year. Carlos was overwhelmed when Tom took him into the big bus and let him sit in the driver's seat. He seemed afraid at first but when he grabbed the steering wheel he got excited and giggled. When Tom helped him blow the horn it scared him, but after a few times the loud noise didn't startle him. During the course of his visit, they spent fun times together on the bus, and this helped them become good buddies.

Close friends of ours, Bruce and Peggy, came to visit and brought Carlos a foot-long, red toy truck that he loved. We gave him a red baseball cap and he wore it all the time. Tom made a walking stick just the right size for Carlos. It was cute to see them talking and strolling side by side with their walking sticks.

When the driver came to pick him up, Carlos cried a lot and didn't want to leave. It was difficult to say goodbye. After we shared hugs and kisses and gave him snacks to take along, he calmed down. As they drove away it was hard to hold back the tears. It was such a fun-filled experience to have this lovable child with us for an extended period of time.

I'm glad Tom took pictures of the foster children. I put them into a photo album. Whenever we take time to look at the pictures, it brings back pleasant memories.

Chapter 19

Opportunities Galore

DURING SOME OF the years I spent as a stay-at-home mom, I volunteered to coordinate a children's group at our church for ages four to eight. Tom assisted me. We set up weekly schedules for volunteers, including ourselves, to conduct children's church during the regular church service. Karen and Michele helped us.

Typically, we sang songs and taught lessons from the Bible or Christian books for children. We asked questions about the lessons, and many of the children were eager to answer. For volunteers who didn't feel comfortable leading songs, we did that portion of the service for them. Tom played the guitar and Karen the organ as Michele and I led songs. Some songs had motions to go along with the singing. One of the children's favorites was parading around the room following us and marching to the song, "When the Saints Go Marching in."

As we gained experience, we introduced new activities to keep the children interested and attentive. Periodically, Karen and Michele put on puppet shows and wrote their own scripts to teach valuable lessons, such as being kind to one another. On occasion, Karen and a friend from youth group, Teresa, dressed up as clowns with colorful costumes and makeup and did miming (using descriptive gestures and actions without words) to help the children learn about the Bible.

The kids liked it when we dressed up in costumes and acted out Bible stories. For example, Karen dressed up as David and Tom as

Goliath. After they both recited their lines and David killed Goliath, a five-year-old boy stood up, pointed at Tom lying on the floor, and said, "Look! He's not dead, he's still breathing."

Something else the children liked was the writing and coloring contests we had from time to time. We set up age-appropriate groups to make it fair, and there was a first, second, and third prize for each group. Everyone else got a consolation prize, so no one was left out.

There were times in the fall and spring when we had parties in our home for the kids. We had a great time playing games and having refreshments. It was a nice way to interact and have fun with the children outside of church. Tom and I enjoyed our eight years working in the children's ministry.

When Karen and Michele were teenagers, I decided to look for part-time work outside the home. I got an office job at a local department store as an inventory control clerk. It was a great benefit having a store discount for purchases. I stayed only three months because it wasn't a smoke-free environment.

A short time later, my daughter Karen and I decided to lose weight by joining a local weight loss center. We were determined to follow the program that promoted good eating habits and exercise at least three times a week. It was challenging to keep a record of everything we ate, but it was worth the effort. After meeting my weight loss goal, I trained to become a leader in the program. This helped me overcome my fear of speaking in front of people. It was satisfying to see participants successfully lose weight and feel better about themselves. This job definitely prepared me for my next position at an all-you-can-eat restaurant.

Close to where we live is a smorgasbord restaurant, well-known for its delicious Pennsylvania Dutch cooking. I worked as a dessert bar attendant. My responsibilities included cutting up pies and cakes and filling the ice cream machine and toppings bar. I became familiar with the names of desserts I had never heard of such as red velvet cake, mince meat pie, and dirt pudding. Employee meals were discounted. I looked forward to buying lunch or supper on occasion.

My favorite choices were baked beans, dried corn, and marinated chicken. Even though the desserts were tempting, my weight loss training helped me resist eating too much of the sweet treats during the three years I worked at the dessert bar.

After working in the fast-paced environment of a busy restaurant, I decided to look for other work. I took a sales associate position at a local clothing store. Shopping for clothes has always been appealing to me, so I thought selling them would be enjoyable.

One side of the store had Plus sizes and the other Misses sizes. I greeted customers and asked if I could help them. One afternoon, a lady came into the store and I greeted her. She said, "I went to other stores and none of them had what I liked in my plus size."

I helped her find numerous outfits to try on in the fitting room. She wanted to buy most of them. To my amazement, after ringing everything up, it totaled over nine hundred dollars. After the customer left, one manager said, "That lady must have won the lottery."

Another manager looked at me and jokingly said, "Now we can all go home, since our sales goal has been met for the day."

Needless to say, this was my best sale at the store. After working there a year, I felt it was time to move on.

Next, I worked in the Reading area at an outlet complex, selling clothing to men and women. This location has numerous stores, and buses bring people from out of town. The spring, summer, and fall months are the busiest, which is when I worked there over a six-month period.

My co-workers were pleasant and I liked working there. However, when the buses stopped coming toward the end of fall and business slowed down, I missed the hustle and bustle of the busy season. As a result, I pursued other employment.

I became aware of a job opening close to home from my neighbor, Pat, who worked for a printing company subsidiary. They provided a fulfillment service primarily for medical insurance companies. I applied and started right away. There were about fifty of us compiling medical information packets that included letters and booklets to be put into large manila envelopes. After we attached address labels, we placed the envelopes in postal carrier bins for mailing to customers of insurance companies.

We were free to talk with our co-workers as long as the work was getting done. I worked with friendly and talkative people, which helped the time pass quickly. After six months, I wanted to get back into sales.

I returned to the first clothing store where I had previously worked. However, instead of selling clothing to customers, I was assigned to steam new clothing that arrived before putting it out on the sales floor. I got bored and missed interacting with customers. After four months, I started looking in the newspaper for something else.

I found an ad for a sales position at a luggage store at the same Reading outlet complex where I had previously sold clothing. I was hired to sell luggage clearance items at a temporary store within the complex.

The next day I started work and took a crash course learning about the different features and types of luggage. Within a few days I made good sales. While working here, I bought luggage with wheels for myself, and that Christmas, Tom, Karen, and Michele got the same type of luggage. We were happy to finally graduate to pulling luggage that rolled on wheels rather than carrying the old fashioned kind that weighed a ton.

After the temporary store closed, I found a position with a department store selling shoes at a mall near Reading. My salary was on a commission basis. It was easy to make sales. My main focus was to help customers find what they wanted. If we didn't have their size, I called another store to get it for them. This meant the salesperson I spoke with from the other store would get the commission, which didn't bother me. My goal was to satisfy the customer. When someone asked for a pair of shoes, I brought out all available colors and this often resulted in selling two or three pairs instead of only one. After achieving a high level of sales, I was given a new identification badge that not only had my name on it, but also, "Customer Enthusiasm 1998 Champion."

I would have stayed at this job longer. However, I had to quit after about seven months due to a challenge with my health. It started when I noticed my hands turning blue and getting swollen. The finger joints became very painful and inflamed. Initially, I went to my family doctor, and he prescribed a steroid but it didn't improve the condition. He recommended I see a dermatologist, who put me on another steroid without success. Afterwards, he suspected the problem was possibly related to an auto-immune disease such as lupus, rheumatoid arthritis, angiodema, or scleroderma. Therefore, he sent me for several blood tests and they came back negative. He couldn't give me a diagnosis.

It was close to Christmas, 1998, and my condition was getting progressively worse. I was having great difficulty using my hands for simple tasks such as washing my hair, cooking, and cleaning. Tom helped me a lot. We prayed and asked others to do the same.

I had been soaking my feet regularly in a foot spa after work, since selling shoes kept me on my feet most of the day. One day, Tom said, "When I pray for your hands to get better, I keep getting a strong feeling you should soak your hands in the foot spa with table salt in warm water three times a day."

"I'm desperate for relief, Tom. I'll give it a try."

Within two days of soaking my hands, I saw improvement. After two weeks my hands were noticeably better. After I continued a few more weeks, my hands were completely healed and have been fine ever since. I was overjoyed to have full use of my hands again.

While at home soaking my hands, I read the local school district's newsletter that's mailed periodically to households in our surrounding area. An ad for substitute teachers caught my attention. They were looking for applicants with a Bachelor's degree, and I applied. After completing the required paperwork and bringing a college transcript to the district office, I was available to work on an "as needed" basis to teach kindergarten through sixth grade. The assistant superintendent was pleased to find out I had eight years of experience teaching young children at church. Her enthusiasm encouraged me, as I was about to begin working in a field that I never realized would open up for me.

It was exciting to start getting phone calls to substitute for teachers absent for one or more days. I couldn't believe I had this job. As a young girl I was shy and could never have imagined teaching a classroom full of students.

After arriving at school and reporting to the secretary in the principal's office, I signed in, went to the classroom, and reviewed the plan for the day left by the regular teacher. When the students arrived and sat down, I greeted them and introduced myself. The day started with the pledge of allegiance and a quiet time before proceeding with the plan.

I found teaching rewarding because I realized that teachers play a significant role in shaping and molding their students. My goal was to show I cared about them as a group and as individuals.

When students didn't understand an assignment or math concept, I took extra time to patiently explain it until it made sense. In one third grade class, a Spanish-speaking student from Columbia had started school the previous day. Some students in the class told me that Juan didn't speak English. Two of them asked for my permission to find a book in the library that translated Spanish into English. What they found was perfect for him to start learning our language.

I planned to write Juan a note in his language and give it to him the next time I went back to that school. My daughter Karen had taken Spanish in high school and college. She helped by writing a note for me that welcomed him to the United States. The following week I went to the same school to teach another class and stopped by the third grade to give Juan my note. After reading it, he looked at me and his eyes lit up. He smiled from ear to ear and said, "Gracias."

In one first grade class, the teacher had made eyeglasses out of stiff cardstock paper for each student. As part of the plan for the day, she left me instructions to give them out to everyone. One boy, petite compared to his classmates, came up to me with a sad expression on his face and was ready to cry. The eyeglasses didn't fit properly. I made them fit by using clear tape on the frame and stuck it to his ears. He was happy to wear the glasses like his classmates. To my surprise, just before dismissal, he ran up front and gave me a big hug.

Of course, all my days didn't go quite as smoothly, since teaching includes disciplining students. In the elementary parochial school I attended as a child, I remembered a technique the nuns used for children who misbehaved. They took a sheet of paper and printed on the top line, "I will obey my teacher." The students were required to write the same on each line to the bottom of the page.

It worked for the nuns, so I thought it would be something worthwhile to try. When I used this approach, it was amazing to see how cooperative and responsive most students were. I noticed an improvement in their behavior. One girl in fourth grade begged me to allow her to take the completed paper home to show her parents. As a rule, I didn't hand these papers back to students, but she persisted and asked several times. Therefore, I made an exception. Another girl in sixth grade turned in her paper with a note that stated, "Read the back please." When I turned it over I was happy to see the following with her signature:

Dear Mrs. Barbagallo,

I am very sorry. I was trying to finish my math. I'm very sorry. Will you forgive me? God bless you. You are a good teacher. Jesus loves you.

Working as an elementary substitute teacher was a great experience for two and a half years. Before leaving this job, I met with the principal of the high school in the district to inquire about the possibility of working at the middle and high school level in the future. He was encouraging and suggested I might want to give it a try, since I already had experience as a substitute.

I wasn't quite sure what to do at that point, so I took a break from teaching. A few months later, I saw an ad in the newspaper for an aide at a high school in a different district. I applied and got hired. My assignment was to assist a handicapped sophomore student confined to a motorized wheelchair. This involved meeting him at school in the morning and staying with him during his classes to take notes, since he didn't have full use of his hands. After dismissal, I accompanied him to a school bus that had a wheelchair lift to get him on the bus. This job lasted about three months. He left school to have surgery and then had an extended recovery at home before returning to school. It was a pleasure to help this young man, who was positive and intelligent.

After working as an aide, I decided to pursue substitute teaching in middle and high school at the same district where I had previously been employed. It was a big change from elementary school, but my earlier experience in teaching gave me the confidence I needed for this new environment. What a wonderful opportunity to be involved in a variety of subjects. My favorites were English, Spanish, and French. Others I liked included music, business, reading, and special education. In each class, my main focus was to get through everything addressed on the plan left by the regular teacher.

The plans were usually easy to follow, which helped me clearly explain assignments to students. Some plans scheduled me to monitor students in the cafeteria during lunch or in study hall. When time permitted, I read inspiring quotations collected from different sources such as Reader's Digest, Guideposts, and Family Circle.

I wanted to encourage and motivate students, if even in a small way, to be positive and successful in their lives. One high school girl said her favorite quote was, "Falling down does not make you a failure, but staying down does." Another young lady told me the one she liked best was, "Two things are bad for the heart—running up stairs and running down people." A guy said that a quote he liked was, "Don't be afraid of pressure. Remember that pressure is what turns a lump of coal into a beautiful diamond."

In one instance, a student gave me a magnetic memo pad with a picture on the cover of a lovely sunrise over a lake. The cover included the words, "Every Day is a Gift!" On the first page of the memo pad, she wrote a note that said, "Thank you for everything you shared with us. It really meant a lot." Underneath, she drew a cute picture of a girl with a big smile.

When it came to substituting for English and foreign languages, I felt comfortable in these classes from the start. My interest in languages began when I was a young child and continued from that time. As I was learning English, my parents taught me Hungarian, and in high school I studied French and Latin.

On one occasion in a French class, we watched a Spiderman movie in French with English subtitles. It was interesting and fast-moving, and to my delight it held the attention of the students for the entire period. What an easy class for me!

In a science class, the plan required me to show a film about evolution using a projector and screen. Before I started the film, a student raised his hand and asked, "Do I have to watch it? I don't believe in evolution."

"We all have to watch it, since it's part of the teacher's plan for the day," I replied.

Shortly after I started the film, the projector smoked, sizzled, and then died. I called the science department and told someone what had happened. A teacher came to pick up the projector. Obviously, it was the end of that portion of the plan for the remaining science classes that day.

At the high school, students have four minutes between periods to go from one class to the next. Walking in the jam-packed corridors as the students hurry in both directions reminded me of the hustle and bustle of crowds taking the subway during rush hour in New York City.

Speaking of where I was brought up, after I told a high school class their assignment, a girl walked to the front of the room and softly asked me, "Are you from New York City?"

"Yes," I replied.

"My mom is from New York too," she smiled and said. "She talks just like you."

I smiled back and nodded, realizing how much my New York accent still stands out after being away from New York for over thirty years.

After leaving the nuclear power industry, Tom found employment working part-time at a home improvement center in the receiving department. He enjoyed interacting with co-workers and truck drivers. While working there, he answered an ad in the newspaper. A rest stop travel plaza along the Pennsylvania Turnpike was advertising for help at its concession stands. It was a part-time job working daytime hours with weekends off.

When people came to order meals, Tom greeted them cheerfully. If it wasn't too busy, he had time to chat with customers while they waited for their food.

One day a young man in his early twenties stood at Tom's counter and asked, "What do you have to eat that's cheap and will fill me up?" He mentioned that he had just left the military and was driving home with a trailer behind his vehicle, and that he inadvertently went east instead of west on the turnpike for quite a distance before realizing it. Now he was headed in the right direction but his concern was not to run out of money before arriving home in Indiana.

After listening to him, Tom felt the guy was on the level and replied, "I'll make you a hearty meal and I'll pay for it."

133

The fellow had a shocked look. "I can't believe you'll do this for me," he said. "Thank you so much."

"I'm glad to help you out."

While the young man was having his meal, Tom stopped by his table and they introduced themselves. The man's name was Paul. They talked a few minutes and exchanged phone numbers. Paul planned to call and let Tom know when he arrived home. Within a few days, they spoke on the phone, and Paul thanked Tom again for the free meal. He mentioned his plans to study for the ministry at Moody Bible Institute and said that he would never forget what Tom did to help him.

Another time, Tom went outside the travel plaza to have lunch and sat at a picnic table where a gentleman was sitting. The other tables were full. He looked at the man, who appeared to be around fifty-five years old. He had a full, grey beard and wore jeans and a black leather jacket. Tom smiled and asked, "Are you a truck driver?"

"No, I'm a Catholic priest," he responded.

They introduced themselves and that's when Tom met Father Roberto, who explained that he was no longer a parish priest due to circumstances beyond his control. He was returning home after a visit with his therapist.

He shared more about his situation. Tom sensed Father Roberto was distressed and asked, "Can I say a prayer for you right now?"

"Sure," he replied.

Tom could tell the priest was deeply touched after hearing the prayer. His eyes watered and with a smile he said, "Thanks for your prayer. I'm sure God had a purpose in allowing us to meet."

Father Roberto's weekly routine was to stop by the travel plaza for ice cream after meeting with his therapist. He and Tom looked forward to seeing each other again. The following week, Father Roberto stopped by and said, "My therapist was pleased when I told her you prayed for me."

Week after week, Tom and Father Roberto talked for a few minutes. Eventually Tom invited him to visit our church on Sunday and come home afterwards for a meal. He gladly accepted the invitation.

When he came over, we had just started doing respite foster care that weekend for a fourteen-year-old girl. They both liked the church service, and after lunch we spent quality time together. Father Roberto related well with the girl and spoke encouraging words to her. It was a relaxing afternoon with our guests and a great first-time foster care experience.

While working at the travel plaza, Tom saw an ad in the newspaper for school bus drivers, which included free training to get a Class B Commercial Driver's License. He had always wanted to drive a large vehicle so it was an easy decision. After completing the training and passing the written and driving tests, he started working as a part-time driver while continuing to work at the concession stand. When a full-time driving position opened up, he quit the other job.

Tom drove about 185 miles a day. In the morning and afternoon, he transported public high school students to and from two vocational technology schools. Later in the day, he transported non-public elementary school students home.

Tom's goal was to be friendly, kind, and respectful toward the students. From the start of the school year, he made an effort to learn their names and enjoyed greeting them in the morning as they got on the bus. As time permitted before and in between runs, he took time to talk with students to get to know them. He shared positive principles for living, hoping that students would find them encouraging and motivating. Tom did this at the start of the week and it became known as the "Thought for the Week." The following are examples:

- Spend your life uplifting and encouraging people, not putting them down.
- Go out of your way to treat others as you want them to treat you.
- Make it a goal to always be honest and make good on your promises.
- Be as kind and considerate with your family as you are with your friends.

Each school year, Tom received positive comments from several students regarding these thoughts. When some were absent on Monday, they would ask on Tuesday morning, "What's the thought for the week?"

During the early years of bus driving, Tom had a local specialty shop make a wooden plaque. It measured eighteen inches long by three inches high and each letter was cut by machine into the wood. The words that he chose were "YOU ARE SPECIAL." The letters were painted black and stood out against the plaque's natural wood-grain finish.

He displayed it below the windshield, visible for everyone to see as they got on and off the bus. Sometimes students made favorable comments about the sign. For example, Tom heard statements like, "Look, it says that I'm special," or "I'm special because the sign says so."

One school year, when Tom arrived at the high school in the morning to wait for students to board the bus, one senior always got there much earlier than anyone else. Tom looked forward to his arrival. They got along well and could talk freely about what was going on in their lives. After a number of months the boy mentioned his intention to quit school. Tom was surprised and tried to encourage him to hang in there and graduate. Unfortunately, the boy was having a difficult time in school. He planned to finish his education taking online computer classes.

After he left school, Tom missed their early morning talks and thought about contacting him to find out how he was doing. Sometime later, he decided to send this former student a card with a personal note. Here is an excerpt:

> Hi…, Hope all is going well for you. I miss having you on my bus and our early morning conversations. I really appreciated how well-behaved you were as my passenger! I want to encourage you… When you get a chance, let me know how you are doing. You're in my thoughts and prayers regularly…

Tom mailed the card on Wednesday, and early Friday morning the boy and his girlfriend were standing on the sidewalk as Tom drove up to his usual parking spot at the high school. The boy smiled and held up the card as Tom got off the bus, and they gave each other a big hug. He introduced his girlfriend, and they talked about his future plans, which sounded promising. Tom was pleased to hear that things were going well for him.

At the end of the school year, it was always an exciting time for students. The majority of students on Tom's bus were seniors who would soon graduate. There was great anticipation in the air on the last day of school. At the end of his seventh year of driving, Tom decided to write a farewell speech to encourage those who were graduating. It was well received, so he continued to do it his last two years of driving. After announcing the title, "As You Graduate," the following is what he said:

> "You have waited for this time that is finally here. A chapter of your life that is ending, and the start of many new things to come. As you look back in future years to this place in time, a distant memory high school will become. Many opportunities, challenges, and choices will be yours to make along life's journey.
>
> Three things to always remember and hold close to your heart— don't give up, don't give up, don't give up. Keep on keeping on, even when your life's circumstances are not always the way you want them to be. Strive for being the kind of person that will be a blessing to those around you. Be open to the work of God in your lives and allow Him to be your life's partner. As you surrender your lives to Him, you will be richly blessed. He will lead and guide you in all things.
>
> I wish each of you the very best in your future years, and you will continue to be in my prayers. Congratulations, God bless you, and remember that You Are Special like the sign says."

He shared the speech that morning with two groups of students. The second group responded with loud cheering and clapping. One student remained on the bus after everyone left and approached Tom with a big smile, shook his hand, and said, "Thanks. I appreciated what you shared. It meant a lot to me."

Tom found this job fulfilling, since most students were well-behaved and a pleasure to have on the bus. Occasionally he received encouraging notes and cards from students and parents.

As a homemaker and full-time mom when we moved from New Hampshire to Pennsylvania in August 1971, I could never have imagined the diversity of jobs that Tom and I would experience in the future.

Chapter 20

Kindred Spirits

THERE'S A FAMILIAR expression, "And they lived happily ever after." As nice as this sounds, it usually doesn't happen in real life. Tom and I loved each other deeply but had to make adjustments after getting married. We needed to learn how to handle differences and emotions in a positive and healthy way. At times, it was challenging to communicate without becoming angry and causing hard feelings.

Early in our marriage while living in Vermont, we saw a movie that promoted the idea that if you're in love, you don't need to say you're sorry. We had never heard that before and decided to give it a try. After a short time, we concluded it didn't work for us.

After five years of marriage, I began to feel we should get counseling from a pastor where we had previously attended church. When I first approached Tom, I came across in a demanding way and he wasn't interested.

Within a week, I brought up the subject again after dinner one evening. As we sat on the couch chatting, I looked at Tom tenderly and gently said, "Sweetheart, I know we get along well, but I think we can learn to communicate better when trying to settle differences. I'm sorry for coming across too strong the last time I approached you about going for counseling."

"Okay, Yolanda. Let me think about it."

The next day, he agreed to go. The first session with Pastor Davis went reasonably well. I looked forward to future sessions.

On the way home after the second session, Tom said, "I'm glad we started meeting with Pastor Davis. I believe we're making progress."

"I feel the same way. I appreciate that you agreed to see him."

"I'm looking forward to the next session, Yolanda."

"Me too."

As a result of our first exposure to counseling, Tom was open to future sessions when they were necessary from time to time.

In most instances, we've learned to resolve differences without going for counseling. Talking about things openly is important to us. The next step is usually to spend time praying together to seek wisdom for dealing with the issue at hand. In opening our hearts to the Lord and listening to each other's prayers, we begin to sense a mutual spirit of compassion, understanding, and love that helps resolve the situation. Sometimes we've found all that's necessary is to say, "I'm sorry."

Over the years, we've discovered that some confrontations and disagreements can be minimized or avoided. The Bible provides guidance and instruction regarding how we're supposed to treat one another. Proverbs 15:1 tells us, "A gentle answer turns away wrath, but a harsh word stirs up anger" (NIV). Galatians 5:22, 23 states, "But the fruit of the Spirit is love, joy, peace, patience, kindness, goodness, faithfulness, gentleness and self control" (NIV).

Whenever Tom and I practice what the Scriptures teach, our relationship tends to thrive and be more fulfilling. As we speak kind and gentle words and express patience, respect, and love, we're less apt to have conflicts. Being polite and considerate with each other has also helped. In addition to how we express ourselves verbally, body language and facial expressions can hinder or promote good communication.

Tom and I don't always agree on everything, since differences are a part of life. We're unique individuals who have become one in marriage, but we still retain unique likes and dislikes. This is a good thing, because it makes life much more interesting.

What helps is to stay focused on listening intently without interrupting while one of us is speaking, which can be challenging at times.

We communicate better when we give each other our full attention. This is something we need to practice continually.

Some of the best conversations we have take place when we go on long walks because we can give each other undivided attention. Tom expressed his feelings in a poem he wrote on June 13, 1999.

Communicating

I love to take walks with my mate
To hold her hand and talk is top rate
We never run out of things to say
And even spend some time to pray.

As we share and truly listen
It lets us know how much we care
To better understand and be understood
Is truly a blessing beyond compare.

Misunderstandings become less and less
As we go the extra mile
And give each other
Our very best.

So no matter what we say
If it's expressed in tenderness and love
Makes all the difference in the world.
Such a relaxing time we have
When we walk and talk and pray.

Another advantage of taking walks regularly is that it's beneficial for our physical and emotional well-being. We find it refreshing and invigorating, and when the sun is shining we get a healthy dose of vitamin D.

An additional healthy pastime we enjoy is weight training. Tom started at thirteen years old and has kept it up all these years. Around the age of seventeen his biceps measured eighteen and three quarter inches, and he was able to do a bicep curl with two hundred and seventy pounds on a barbell. He got me started many years ago and I find myself feeling better after doing the workout program he set up for me.

Along with keeping physically fit, we've spent time studying and learning about nutrition to maintain good health. Our goal is to take the best possible care of ourselves. We want to stay healthy and be around for each other into our twilight years.

When it comes to preparing meals, Tom and I like working together or independently in the kitchen. As a team, one of us takes the lead and the other helps as necessary. We've learned to use spices we weren't familiar with while growing up, such as rosemary, ginger, and cumin. These have enhanced the flavor and nutritional value of stir-fries and soups. We like tasty meals that promote staying healthy.

Before getting married, a meal I had with Tom and his mother was her homemade stuffed pizza, which is similar to stromboli. She learned to make it while growing up in Italy. I loved it and asked her for the recipe. It wasn't until we got married that I made it for the first time. Of course, Tom was delighted and we enjoyed it immensely. He thought it was comparable to what his mother made. This meal became a family favorite.

The procedure for making stuffed pizza is interesting. After the dough rises, I divide it in half to make two loaves and roll them out. Then I layer parmesan cheese, slices of ham, and salami and top them with grated mozzarella cheese. Next, I roll up each loaf and poke holes along the top with a fork to let the steam escape. As the loaves bake, a wonderful aroma fills the house and makes it smell like an Italian restaurant. This delicious meal always disappeared fast when Karen and Michele lived at home.

As my interest in baking progressed, I started making homemade pizza. In preparing the dough, I used the same recipe as for stuffed pizza, except I needed only half the quantity of flour. Besides using tomato sauce and cheese on the pizza, seasoned with basil and oregano, I added toppings such as diced red peppers, mushrooms, onions, and garlic. This was a great family meal that is still popular for Tom and me.

When Tom worked fifteen minutes away, he came home for lunch occasionally. One day after the girls left for school, I called Tom's office and asked, "How would you like to come home for lunch? I'm making pizza."

"Sounds great. I'd love to."

Soon after he arrived and sat down at the table, I took the pizza out of the oven, sliced it, and hurriedly walked over holding the pan. As he looked at the pan up in the air close beside him, he moved his chair backwards to give me room to serve him. I slid the spatula under a slice and moved it toward Tom's plate. The pizza slipped off onto his light blue dress slacks. He jumped out of his seat and yelled, "This hot pizza is burning my legs!"

The pizza dropped onto the kitchen floor. Tom rushed to take off his pants. I exclaimed, "Sweetheart, I'm very sorry."

While Tom stood in his Fruit of the Loom underwear, he said, "That's okay. I know it was an accident."

Instead of having a relaxing lunch, he had to wash up and change while I cleaned up the mess and put his slacks into the washer. Time was running out. He quickly gulped down a slice or two and went back to work. This experience helped us realize how important it is to have a good sense of humor, even when things don't work out as planned. What happened that day still makes us laugh.

Something I love about Tom is that he has a natural talent to be funny. He feels the same about me, so we keep each other laughing. Sometimes when we're talking, one of us doesn't clearly hear the other. When we respond to what we thought we heard, it may have little or nothing to do with what was said. These instances are often comical.

One night we watched an old western movie on TV. We didn't see it from the beginning and hadn't seen it before. Tom commented, "The two starring actors are Marlon Brando and Karl Malden."

"How did you know it was Marlon Brando right away? I didn't recognize him."

Tom was lying on the couch and I sat a few feet behind him in a recliner. He replied, "By his face and voice."

With the TV on and looking at the back of Tom's head, I repeated what I thought I heard. "You recognized him by his face and horse?"

Tom sat up on the couch and turned to look at me. With a big grin on his face, he replied, "I said his face and voice, not face and horse." We laughed hysterically.

There was a period of time during Tom's engineering career when he experienced a five-month layoff. It was after finishing up a long-term assignment as a contractor for a public utility company at a nearby nuclear power plant. When he went back to his company, there wasn't work available for him at the home office. Therefore, he was laid off and collected unemployment benefits. During the week, he worked part-time doing office work at a place that sold and repaired lawn power equipment. He also spent time looking for a job in his field.

I kept busy working thirty hours a week as a dessert bar attendant at a nearby smorgasbord. Tom did a lot of the household chores, such as cooking, cleaning, and washing clothes. One day after I got home from my job, he said, "I never realized how much work you did as a stay-at-home mom."

"I'm glad you can appreciate how much it involves."

"It's a challenge for me to get everything done, Yolanda."

"You're doing a great job, Tom."

It was certainly a pleasure to come home from work and know that Tom was preparing most meals. I taught him how to make homemade pizza, which was a real treat for me since he did all the work. One evening I pulled into the garage and got out of the car. As I opened the door to go upstairs, I smelled the aroma of roasted chicken in the oven. Tom welcomed me with a hug and kiss and said, "Yolanda, sit in the recliner and relax. I'll have everything ready in ten minutes."

"Okay, I can't wait to eat. I'm hungry."

When Tom called me into the kitchen, my mouth watered as I looked at the steaming chicken on a large, white platter, surrounded by roasted potatoes. The meal included a salad and green beans. I said, "What a nice surprise. Everything looks delicious. And the beautiful music and candlelight. You outdid yourself, Tom."

"You deserve it, Yolanda. I appreciate that you're working while I'm hunting for a full-time job."

We enjoyed the scrumptious meal. Normally, I'd clean up after he made dinner. This time Tom said, "Yolanda, go rest and take it easy in the living room. I'll take care of cleaning up."

"Thanks, Tom, for making this a special evening. I'll never forget it."

The company that laid Tom off rehired him to take an assignment as a contractor with the same public utility as before, but this time at their nuclear group office headquarters. After a period of months at this location, he was hired to take a permanent position with the utility company. A few years later, a downsizing occurred that affected Tom's work section. As a result, he was offered and accepted a position at a nuclear power plant one and a half hours from home in Pennsylvania near the Maryland border. It was a tiresome trip daily in good weather, but when it snowed the round trip could total over four hours.

Another downsizing took place, which resulted in Tom's accepting a voluntary separation package. It included severance pay, health benefits for one year, and unemployment compensation.

A company-sponsored career center was available for employees leaving their jobs. Tom attended the sessions during his last six months of employment, because he had to determine what to do next. It was definitely a challenge for him to decide what future occupation to consider.

I wanted to make the transition easier for Tom by making his last six months at the plant worth remembering. I called it a "countdown celebration." Each month I set aside a special day to do something I knew he would enjoy, such as a favorite meal and dessert or treating him out to eat. I surprised him with encouraging greeting cards, helium balloons, and flowers. Tom anticipated each celebration, which helped take his mind off the apprehension he felt about the future.

From a monetary standpoint, the loss of a good paying job for Tom could have been disheartening. However, many years before the downsizing, we attended a seminar that helped us learn to manage money effectively. We became familiar with how to budget, save, and invest for the future, and how to use credit cards wisely.

A helpful concept was presented that we had never heard before. It was learning to wait for what you want and not buying things on impulse. The technique included keeping an ongoing list of items we thought we needed and to include the date of entry for each item. Also, to hold off from buying anything until it was on the list for thirty days. During this period, we were told to ask ourselves questions such as, is the item really needed, is the price reasonable, is it the right timing to make the purchase? The plan emphasized that we'd be amazed a month later at how many items would drop in priority or we wouldn't want them at all. We followed this advice, and to our surprise, crossed off a number of items that we no longer desired.

As a result of the seminar, we became more unified as a couple and better equipped to deal with money issues. We hid nothing from each other, which made it easier to stay focused on financial plans for the future. Being open and honest in this area has definitely improved our relationship. We fully trust each other to make wise choices when it comes to making individual purchases. For big ticket items like cars, appliances, and home furnishings, we shop together and enjoy doing research to get the best deal. We have different strengths. Working as a team has benefited us greatly, and at the same time it's fun and rewarding.

There's always more to learn as far as how to maintain and improve our marriage. In some ways, it's like a car that needs a tune-up to keep it running efficiently.

In the fall of 1984, I was listening to Dr. Canfield, a Christian psychologist, on a local radio station. His program aired Monday through Friday every afternoon. He mentioned an upcoming marriage retreat at his home, which was to take place on a Friday night and Saturday. We had never been to a retreat. I wanted to go and told Tom and he agreed. I called and made reservations and found out that anyone attending from out of town would need to get overnight accommodations at a nearby motel. We were less than an hour away so we commuted.

During his introduction Friday night, Dr. Canfield mentioned that he and his wife had scheduled these retreats at their home in the past and that this would be the last one. After hearing this, we were happy to be there that weekend. He told us that some couples in attendance, whom he had had in counseling sessions, were very close to splitting up. Of course, he singled out none of these couples. He mentioned that this retreat could be the last chance to save their marriages.

On Saturday morning, he asked everyone to make a list of one-line statements about their mates to identify strengths in one column and things that were bothersome in another column. He emphasized the importance of being honest if we expected to achieve good results.

Afterwards, couples were told to go to a private place on the property or to their cars to discuss each item on the list. We sat in the car and talked. It was a worthwhile exercise to see the positive comments and to become aware of what bothered each of us. For the most part, the annoying things were minor in nature and unintentional. Tom and I agreed to make an effort to change behaviors to accommodate each other's wishes.

After a tasty lunch in the Canfield home, Dr. Canfield told couples to meet outside. He explained that an obstacle course was set up on the property for the next activity, which was to test communication skills. A string defined the path of the course. To start with, the husbands had to direct their blindfolded wives verbally to the halfway point. Then they reversed roles to the end of the course. The second half proved to be more challenging. It required some climbing and ducking to avoid hitting obstacles. Consequently, it was harder for the wives to direct their husbands.

After I was blindfolded, Tom got a great idea as to how to direct me through the course. He said, "I'll stand in front of you and give you directions. All you have to do is listen to the sound of my voice and follow where I say to go. Do you understand, Yolanda?"

"Yes,"

"For example, walk to the left or right or straight ahead." He was precise in guiding me and I finished quickly.

When it was my turn to direct him, it didn't go quite as well. The first obstacle was to have him climb over a swing seat and bend his head at the same time to avoid hitting the top of the swing frame. He made it over the seat okay, but banged his head because I failed to tell him to duck ahead of time. As we continued I got him safely around the barbecue pit. The last obstacle was the most challenging. I had to get Tom to approach an unusual looking tree with a wide, short trunk and at least eight low-hanging branches. He had to climb through a V-shaped opening in the trunk. At the same time, I told him which direction to move so he wouldn't hit his head on the branches. Believe it or not, I got Tom through that obstacle without a problem. After he had hit his head earlier on the swing set, I was determined to get him through the rest of the course without additional bruises. He was definitely happy about that.

Tom and I were one of the first couples to finish. We watched the remaining wives lead their husbands through the tree obstacle. Not too many husbands banged their heads on the branches because they got clear instructions from their wives. However, the last couple was an exception, since the wife had a very difficult time communicating to her husband how to climb over the short tree trunk without hitting his head on the branches. It was sad to see the man hit his head at least six times because of his wife's poor instructions. When they finally succeeded, everyone clapped and cheered.

We learned positive and practical ways to improve our relationship, between Dr. Canfield's lectures and participation in the planned activities. This unforgettable and inspiring weekend motivated us to attend marriage retreats over the years.

As Tom and I think back to when we got married in 1969, it's hard to believe how quickly the years have gone by. We look forward to celebrating each anniversary.

We were deeply touched in 1985 when Karen was fourteen and Michele was eleven years old. They began a tradition on our sixteenth wedding anniversary by preparing dinner in a romantic setting with candlelight and soft music. Afterwards, they entertained us, taking turns playing the piano and then putting on a puppet show together. This tradition of anniversary celebrations continued for many years. One year, the girls made fettuccini Alfredo with a salad and herb bread. Dessert was strawberry shortcake. We certainly appreciated their efforts to make us feel special.

We are grateful to have learned how to improve and maintain our relationship throughout our married life. We continually strive to keep it vibrant and fulfilling, with a determination to have a good attitude and cheerful disposition as we relate to each other. Even as we get older, our desire is to stay young at heart, have fun times, and laugh a lot. Life is too short. We want to cherish each day together and anticipate many more precious moments in the future.

Chapter 21

Entertaining Memories

*A*S TOM AND I reflect back over the years, we have many wonderful and vivid memories. Whenever we think of the fun and amusing times as a family, it warms our hearts and makes us smile.

It was enjoyable taking walks as a family on our country road. Unfortunately, some people throw trash from their vehicles and litter accumulates alongside the road. Occasionally, Tom would point at empty soda cans, fast food wrappers, and Styrofoam coffee cups. He'd say, "What a bunch of slobs, who throw trash out their car windows."

After several walks and hearing her Dad's comment a few times, Karen pointed to a soda can and yelled, "Daddy, look at that slob over there!"

"Karen, the can isn't the slob," he replied with a smile. "The person who threw it there is the slob."

"The next time we walk, let's bring a trash bag and clean up this mess," I said.

"That's a good idea, Yolanda."

Tom and I had talked with the girls about when we lived in New York City and how we ended up living in the country. He mentioned, "Mom and I were city slickers and now we're country bumpkins."

A few weeks later, Michele had a girlfriend visiting and they talked while playing in the living room. Tom and I were in the kitchen preparing a meal. We overheard Michele say, "My mommy and daddy were sicky slivers and now they're country bumpkins." Tom and I chuckled.

Shortly after I met Tom, he surprised me when he said, "I'm wearing a hairpiece."

"I can't tell you're wearing one."

"I use hairspray to keep it well-groomed."

By the time we moved into our house, Tom was wearing his fourth hairpiece, which was getting old. It needed replacement. He approached me and said, "With the expenses in owning a home, I'm not sure whether to buy another hairpiece because they're very costly. In fact, I'm thinking about not wearing one any longer."

"I think you'd look terrific without one. And you wouldn't have to spend time every week removing it from your head to clean it. It's time-consuming to maintain the hairpiece."

"You're right, Yolanda. I'm going to take it off for good."

Tom took his hairpiece off on a Saturday. That Sunday while walking into the small country church we attended, the pastor's wife, Helen, smiled and greeted us as we walked in the door. She looked at Tom and said enthusiastically, "You look great. I love your natural look!"

"Thank you, Helen."

Other church members also expressed how they liked his new look.

With the positive comments he received, Tom couldn't wait to go to work on Monday to see the reaction of his co-workers.

He arrived at the office earlier than usual and sat at his desk. The first person Tom saw was Kathy, the department secretary. Her desk was in a position where they could see each other. When he said good morning, she looked at Tom and rubbed her eyes. With a shocked expression on her face, she cried out, "What happened to your hair?"

"I wore a hairpiece and decided to take it off," Tom replied nonchalantly.

When Steve, the department manager, arrived and saw Tom, his face turned white and his eyes bulged. He exclaimed, "Tom, what made your hair fall out? Did something traumatic happen over the weekend?"

While working at his desk, Tom overheard someone ask Kathy, "Who's the new guy sitting at Tom's desk?"

One co-worker told another secretary that Tom lost a football bet and had to shave his head, and she believed him.

The reaction from co-workers varied. Some asked Tom what happened while others didn't say anything. To say the least, Tom was having a blast and thoroughly enjoying himself. That afternoon he was scheduled to attend a meeting with five co-workers. Tom arrived and no one commented about his new appearance. In fact, everyone was serious and focused on the business at hand. During a lull in the discussion, Tom felt it was time to break the ice and set everyone at ease. He looked at one of the men and blurted out, "Hey, Walt, can I borrow your comb?"

That's all it took to get them laughing hysterically. By this time, Tom was having so much fun that he wished he had taken the hairpiece off much sooner!

A week before Tom removed his hairpiece, I bought ten cans of his favorite men's hairspray, which was on sale at the supermarket. I couldn't resist such a good bargain. However, since he would no longer need the hairspray, I returned it to the store. The customer service lady asked, "Why are you retuning ten cans of hairspray?"

"My husband no longer needs it. He stopped wearing his hairpiece after I bought the cans."

"Are you for real?" she asked with a frown.

"Yes, I am."

She went and talked with a manager, came back, and gave me a full refund.

One week after Tom stopped wearing the hairpiece, he and Karen were taking a walk along the road and holding hands. She was four years old and had beautiful, waist-length hair. Out of the blue, she asked, "Daddy, can I have my hair the same way you have it?"

"No. Karen, it wouldn't look good on you!"

She accepted his response and they smiled at each other. He felt very loved and admired because she wanted to have his hairstyle, which was hair around the sides and back of the head with a large bald spot on top!

One Thanksgiving as we sat around the table stuffing ourselves with turkey and all the trimmings, we enjoyed conversation about our favorite parts of the turkey. Karen was seven at the time. Michele was four years old. Tom asked Karen, "What's your favorite part of the turkey?"

"I like the legs. They're the best," Karen replied with a smile.

"What about you, Michele?" Tom asked, "What's your favorite part of the turkey?"

"The chicken!" Michele replied excitedly.

We laughed merrily at Michele's precious response.

"Do you mean the white meat, Michele?" I asked.

"Yes, mommy."

During these early years, we had a male cat named Smokey as part of the family. Our neighbor, Shirley, gave him to Karen as a kitten when she turned four years old. He had white fur with lightly-shaded orange stripes. Smokey was friendly and glad to be around us. Even though he spent most of the time outdoors, we had fun times with him indoors.

As he got older, it was humorous when Karen and Michele dressed him up with hats, my dark brown, long-haired wig, and Tom's red velvet bow tie. Smokey never seemed to mind one bit. Often, Tom would lie down on the carpet on his side with his head propped on his arm while watching TV. Smokey always climbed onto his hip, stretched out, and fell asleep. During the winter, one of his favorite places to lie around was in the black metal log carrier by the warm, cozy wood stove in the kitchen.

I noticed the Sunday newspaper occasionally had pictures and stories of pets. As a family, we talked about how neat it would be to see Smokey in the newspaper. When Karen was nine years old, she submitted a picture of Smokey in the log carrier along with a story. Sometime later, a reporter called from the newspaper and scheduled an interview with Karen at our home to find out more about Smokey. During his visit, Smokey hung around the reporter and acted as if he were being interviewed instead of Karen.

A few weeks later, I sat in the living room reading the Sunday paper. Tom was downstairs. Karen and Michele were playing in their bedroom. I screamed at the top of my lungs. Tom rushed upstairs and the girls ran to the living room. "What happened? Are you okay?" Tom asked frantically.

"Look, look at the paper!" I shouted.

Karen and Michele jumped up and down when they saw Smokey's picture. Karen yelled, "That's my story!"

"I can't believe Smokey's in the newspaper!" Michele squealed.

"Now Smokey's a celebrity," Tom added.

The caption under Smokey's picture stated, "Just the Cat's Meow," with the following story:

Karen Barbagallo wrote to the Sunday Family Living Section about her cat and even sent this photo along. Smokey, a mice-hunting cat, lives with her family. He used to bring home animals, Karen said.

"At first my mom bought ammonia but our cat still kept putting his animals on the mat," Karen said. "Then my mom bought some pine oil. It worked! Now our cat doesn't bring home animals and put them on the mat."

One of Smokey's favorite places to rest is in the wood carrier; another favorite location is in the iron pot in the kitchen.

Smokey eats anything he can get – except things that are good for you like fruit. As a matter of fact, she wrote, "If it wasn't for him, we'd have hundreds of mice!"

(Used by permission – Reading Eagle Company)

When Karen and Michele were youngsters, they sold greeting cards to our neighbors and friends. It was through a company that promoted the sale of cards by children using their catalogue. The amount of sales determined the prizes that could be won. Karen and Michele got things like games, a remote control car, and a telescope.

Before attempting to sell cards, the girls practiced their sales approach at home with me. I pretended to be our next door neighbor, Rose. They would greet me and say, "Hi, Rose, how are you? Would you like to look at this catalogue and buy some greeting cards?"

"Yes, I'd be glad to. Let me see what you have," I responded with a big smile.

They practiced until they felt comfortable and ready to sell cards, and the first customer was always Rose. She was such a kind and friendly neighbor. Of course, she couldn't resist buying cards. This first sale was a big encouragement to our girls, and it helped them develop confidence in making future sales. Fortunately, Karen and Michele are three years apart in age, so they didn't bombard Rose at the same time.

Prior to getting married, I didn't do any baking because my mom had done it. She made everything from scratch. I thoroughly enjoyed all the things she made, such as peach pie, raisin bread, and Hungarian pastries. Shortly after becoming a wife, I learned how to bake. Tom loved what I made and always complimented me.

I baked frequently after moving to Lancaster County. My family got used to having homemade desserts. It was more work to start from scratch like Mom did, but it was worth the time, since Tom and the girls appreciated my efforts. I baked some desserts my mom had made and also others like peanut butter pie, cheesecake, and strawberry shortcake with homemade whipped cream. I felt right at home living in Pennsylvania Dutch country where people are known for their delicious baked goods.

Tom worked with a friend, Chander, who had a vegetable garden in his backyard. One of the items he had grown was rhubarb, which has long stalks and large leaves. He gave Tom a bunch of stalks with leaves and told him that it could be used to make rhubarb pie. Neither Tom nor I could remember ever seeing it when we lived in New York City. If we did see it there or in a Pennsylvania grocery store, we didn't know what it was since it was unfamiliar to us.

With my experience in baking, I felt confident I could make the pie with the directions in my cookbook. After preparing it there was enough for two pies. I kept one and gave the other to our babysitters' mom for her family to enjoy. That night we couldn't wait to try this new kind of pie that we never had before.

The girls and I took one bite. "This pie is bitter, Mommy," said Karen, with a sour look on her face.

"Mommy, I don't like this pie," Michele added.

"You don't have to eat it. I don't like it either," I replied.

For Tom, it was a different story. He said, "I like the homemade pie crust. The filling is tart, but maybe that's how rhubarb pie is supposed to taste."

Tom finished his piece. The next morning before going to work, he had another piece of pie for breakfast. While I was half asleep waiting for the girls to get up for school, he came into the bedroom and said, "The pie didn't taste as strong this morning. It's probably because it was refrigerated overnight."

That morning after the girls were picked up by the school bus, I received a call from our neighbor, Mrs. Horst. I had given her the extra pie. She asked, "Yolanda, did you use the rhubarb leaves instead of the stalks to make the pie filling?"

"Yes," I replied.

"Did you know the leaves are poisonous?"

"No, I didn't."

"I realized you made a mistake and didn't serve it to my family."

"I'm very sorry, Mrs. Horst."

"That's okay, Yolanda."

When I got off the phone, I was concerned about Tom since he had eaten two pieces of pie. I panicked and rushed to call him at work. The first good sign was that he answered the phone with his usual greeting, "Hello, Tom Barbagallo, QA."

What a big relief to find out he was okay. I informed him about what our neighbor had told me. He said, "I had pain in my stomach at work, so I took antacid tablets a co-worker gave me. Now I'm feeling better."

We found out later that rhubarb stalks are sold without leaves in the supermarket. When Tom mentioned to Chander what happened, he felt bad about not removing the leaves.

That evening after the girls went to bed, Tom and I looked in my cookbook and discovered that it assumed the rhubarb leaves were previously removed from the stalks and discarded before preparing the filling. I guess the directions would have been sufficient for someone familiar with how to use rhubarb. Obviously, I wasn't one of those people.

"Don't feel bad, Yolanda," Tom said. "From the recipe, I wouldn't have known either to use the stalks rather than the leaves."

"That makes me feel a little bit better."

Tom took me in his arms, looked at me, smiled, and asked, "What did you do with the rhubarb stalks?"

"I gave them to Karen and Michele." I smiled. "They had fun playing with the stalks in the backyard while I was busy preparing the leaves for filling."

Tom laughed hysterically and I joined in!

During their teen years, Karen and Michele took an interest in baking. One of the favorites I taught them to make is a Pennsylvania Dutch recipe for apple crisp. This dessert doesn't have a pie crust and it's quick and easy to prepare. The basic ingredients are sliced apples, sugar, and cinnamon, which is mixed with water and flour. The topping is a mixture of rolled oats, butter, and sugar. An option is to sprinkle extra cinnamon on top.

One time when Michele made this dessert it tasted different from usual. She had accidentally sprinkled chili powder on top instead of cinnamon, since both spice shakers were identical in color and size. It was disappointing because our mouths were watering for this scrumptious treat. To try and salvage it, Michele attempted to scrape off the top coating of chili powder, but it was impossible to remove completely. After a taste, Tom, Karen, and I didn't want to have anymore. However, Michele was determined not to let it go to waste, so she had it all for herself.

Years ago I started collecting rubber stamps to use on cards, letters, and envelopes. Tom liked using them too. A favorite of mine is a smiley face. Some of the other stamps are, "May God's Love Brighten Your Day" and "You're Beary Special."

In April, when Tom prepared to mail a tax payment to the Internal Revenue Service, he stamped the back of the envelope. He put it on a living room end table, since it was ready for mailing. I looked at the back of the envelope to see what stamp he used. It was quite a surprise. I showed it to him. We couldn't stop laughing. By mistake he grabbed, "I Miss You," enclosed within a flowered heart, and Tom stamped it with my lavender inkpad instead of his red one. I guess Uncle Sam needed to know that someone out there really did miss him!

When telephone answering machines first came out, Tom and I were reluctant to get one. It didn't seem necessary. However, we bought one when Tom was job hunting due to a layoff. He wanted to make sure he didn't miss any calls for possible employment opportunities.

The machine had another advantage because we could leave each other personal voice memos. It took time to get used to it becoming a part of our daily lives. Afterwards, it seemed like one of those conveniences we couldn't do without.

One afternoon soon after purchasing the answering machine, I decided to leave Tom my first personal memo to listen to when he got home from work. I said, "Hi, Sweetheart, I made salads for us. They're on the bottom shelf in the refrigerator. I'm going on a bike ride and I'll see you later. If you get home before I do and you're hungry, go ahead and have your salad."

I got home before Tom and we had our salads together. I didn't mention anything about leaving him a memo.

Two days later, he called me from work and I wasn't home. Instead of hearing our usual answering machine greeting, he was shocked to hear my voice talking about a salad and going biking. He was confused to say the least. When Tom got home from work, he asked, "Yolanda, would you please listen to the answering machine greeting?"

I couldn't believe what I was hearing. "Tom, how did that happen?"

"When you went to push the memo button, you pressed the greeting button by mistake since they're close to each other." Tom smiled. "The original greeting for callers got replaced with your memo for me."

We cracked up laughing. Consequently, anyone who called heard a greeting that made no sense. They may have wondered if all was well at the Barbagallos'. We shared this episode with friends and they thought it was hilarious. One mentioned about being disappointed she didn't call to hear the unusual greeting.

Our daughter Karen and her husband, Richard, were blessed with identical twin boys, Benjamin and Jonathan. As grandparents, it has been a joy spending time with the boys regularly. When they were between one and a half and two years old, amusing things occurred that we'll never forget.

Tom and Karen sat side by side at the kitchen table while she typed the manuscript for this book from handwritten pages that Tom and I had prepared for each chapter. One day, what happened next turned out to be a frequent occurrence while they worked together.

During a break from typing, Tom remained seated at the table while the boys wanted to play with him. He got a great idea. Tom looked at the grandsons and said, "Benjamin and Jonathan, go stand at the kitchen closet door. I'll call your name and you can take turns running to Grandpa."

The boys ran quickly to the door at the opposite end of the kitchen and waited with anticipation. First Tom looked at Benjamin and said, "Okay, Benjamin, you go first and then Jonathan will go next." Tom grabbed magnetic plastic numbers one, two, and three from the refrigerator door. He held up each number as he called it out, first for Benjamin, then for Jonathan. "One! Two! Three! Go!"

At the sound of "go," Benjamin and Jonathan took turns racing across the kitchen. Each would take off running from the closet door, across the kitchen, past the long rectangular kitchen table toward Grandpa. Then they'd bolt around the first corner of the table and round the corner where Tom was sitting. Finally, they'd squeal with glee as they barreled into Grandpa's arms for a huge bear hug. Then, back they ran across the kitchen to the closet door, waiting for Grandpa to call them again.

On any given day, they ran to Tom over and over. One day it turned out to be a marathon. Tom decided to count the number of times they ran to him. Between Benjamin and Jonathan, it was a total of ninety-five times. Grandpa and the boys were exhausted and ready to collapse.

Karen's mother-in-law, Audrey, came from the Scranton, Pennsylvania, area for an extended visit around Mother's Day. At Karen and Richard's place, the three of us moms enjoyed celebrating the holiday together. After we opened gifts, there was a large accumulation of wrapping paper on the living room floor.

Benjamin and Jonathan were wearing identical shirts with Hawaiian style blue and green flowers on a beige background. As Tom sat on the couch, he called out, "Hey, boys, come here to Grandpa."

They ran and stood in front of him. Tom started stuffing their shirts with crumpled wrapping paper. "You're going to have lots of fun, boys," he said. "Wait until I'm finished."

Benjamin and Jonathan giggled as Grandpa overstuffed their shirts until it looked like the buttons would pop off. The boys started shouting excitedly and running back and forth from the kitchen into the living room non-stop. It looked as if watermelons were under their shirts. They yelled and laughed while running, bumping into, and bouncing off each other.

Karen, Richard, Audrey, Tom, and I laughed hysterically as we watched Benjamin and Jonathan having such a fabulous time. It was obvious that our laughter helped keep the boys motivated to continue entertaining themselves and us. What a memorable and delightful time!

Epilogue

TOM AND I couldn't have anticipated the series of stormy events that we'd go through before and after getting married, and the way circumstances would spiral out of control. The unexpected period of separation as newlyweds was devastating. However, after being reunited, a beautiful rainbow started to appear on the horizon of our lives. Despair turned to hope. The time came for us to experience new, exciting, and life-changing adventures, one of which led to an awesome discovery. Rather than just hoping we'd get to heaven someday, Tom and I were thrilled to learn we could be absolutely certain because of what the Bible teaches.

The more we studied the Bible, the more it became clear that God's desire is for everyone to know His plan of salvation. We learned that the devil, Satan, is real and that his strategy is to lead people away from God. His primary goal is to do everything he can to make sure that people don't become aware of God's wonderful plan for their lives.

Some people may think it's not important to know their eternal destiny while they're alive. Others may feel it's impossible to be certain of their final destination after death. Of course, there are those who are not sure but hopeful about going to heaven, as it was for Tom and me.

As I reflect back to an earlier time in my life, I had a misconception of the devil and pictured him as a harmless and humorous character in a red suit with a large pitchfork. I remember hearing people say, "I want to go to hell because that's where all my friends will be." This statement didn't scare me back then, but now it frightens me. After getting into the Bible, I found Scriptures that made me aware of the devil and his evil works. For example, it says in 1 Peter 5:8, "Be careful—watch out for attacks from Satan, your great enemy. He prowls around like a hungry lion looking for some victim to tear apart." Another verse that makes reference to him is in Ephesians 6:11, "Put on all of God's armor so that you will be able to stand safe against all strategies and tricks of Satan."

We discovered that God's plan of salvation was never meant to be complicated. The gospel message in the New Testament is spelled out clearly so that ordinary people like us can understand it. God's love is awesome. Once we accept His offer, it's like finding a pot of gold at the end of a rainbow, but even better because it has eternal value. How extraordinary to realize why Jesus sacrificed His life for us! Shedding His blood, dying on the cross, and rising from the dead was for our benefit so we could experience eternal life. In 1 Peter 3:18, the Bible states, "Christ died once for the sins of all us guilty sinners, although He Himself was innocent of any sin at any time, that He might bring us safely home to God." The Scriptures make it clear that we are all sinners, as stated in Romans 3:23, "For all have sinned and fall short of the glory of God" (NIV).

It was an eye opener for Tom and me to recognize we were not only sinners in need of God's forgiveness, but also that we had to repent—or turn away from—doing what the Bible points out as sin. For example, this includes lying, cheating, and stealing. As we learned, being sincerely repentant means shifting away from sinful behavior. Keeping this in mind makes sin less appealing and motivates us to practice what the Scriptures teach about living for God.

What's amazing is that the Bible not only addresses the sinful condition of humanity, but also makes provision to rescue us and redirect our lives, resulting in peace with God and everlasting life. A Scripture that makes this apparent is in Romans 6:23, "For the wages of sin is death, but the free gift of God is eternal life through Jesus Christ our Lord." Salvation is not something we earn by doing good works, because it is a free gift that is based upon His grace (unmerited favor) toward us. This is clearly explained in Ephesians 2:8–9, "For it is by grace you have been saved, through faith – and this not from yourselves, it is the gift of God – not of works so that no one can boast" (NIV). In reality, it's all about God's mercy, grace, and love. His desire is for us to spend eternity with Him, but it's our choice to accept or reject His offer.

When we say yes to God and receive His free gift, it is an act of faith to believe and trust in Jesus Christ for salvation. Asking Him to forgive our sins, wanting to turn away from sinful behavior, and accepting what Jesus did on the cross as payment for our sins is the key to receiving eternal life.

For anyone who has the desire to accept His free gift, you can pray with a sincere heart like Tom and I did while watching a minister on television. Here is something similar to what we prayed:

Dear God,

I realize that I am a sinner. Please forgive me as I repent (turn away) from my sins. Thank you for sending Jesus to sacrifice His life by dying on the cross to pay the penalty for my sins. I turn my life over to You completely. Thank you for the free gift of eternal life. Please take control of every area of my life so I can live in a way that pleases You. Amen.

The certainty of knowing our eternal destiny in heaven is confirmed in the following Scriptures:

"I have written this to you who believe in the Son of God so that you may know you have eternal life."
—1 John 5:13

"For God so loved the world so much that He gave His only Son [Jesus] so that anyone who believes in Him shall not perish but have eternal life."
—John 3:16

"My sheep recognize my voice, and I know them, and they follow me. I give them eternal life and they shall never perish. No one shall snatch them away from me."
—John 10:27–28

"I say emphatically that anyone who listens to my message and believes in God who sent me has eternal life, and will never be damned for his sins, but has already passed out of death into life."

—John 5:24

"Jesus told her, 'I am the one who raises the dead and gives them life again. Anyone who believes in me, even though he dies like anyone else, shall live again. He is given eternal life for believing in me and shall never perish.'"

—John 11:25–26

As we're committed to following God and putting Him first, we can experience a new beginning that will affect every area of our lives. As it says in 2 Corinthians 5:17, "Therefore, if anyone is in Christ, he is a new creation; the old has gone, the new has come!" (NIV). Also in Ephesians 4:23, 24, it states, "to be made new in the attitude of your minds; and to put on the new self, created to be like God in true righteousness and holiness" (NIV).

For anyone who is unfamiliar with the Bible, a good place to begin is to read the gospel of John, which is helpful in providing a good understanding of Jesus' life and God's plan of salvation. Additionally, to grow in our relationship with God, it's helpful to read the Bible regularly to learn how He wants us to live. A Scripture addressing this is found in 2 Timothy 3:16, "The whole Bible was given to us by inspiration from God and is useful to teach us what is true and to make us realize what is wrong in our lives; it straightens us out and helps us to do what is right."

Attending Sunday services to praise God in song and to hear the Bible being taught adds to our spiritual understanding and growth. In addition, some churches set aside an evening during the week for Bible study and prayer. Other churches may have small groups like ours where people meet regularly in homes. These groups usually sing Christian songs and study the Bible. Afterwards, there's a time to pray for individual needs and then time for socializing. With all the challenges that are part of our lives, meeting with others is encouraging and helpful in maintaining a close relationship with the Lord.

Another aspect of our spiritual walk that makes a positive difference is praying daily. For example, we can say memorized prayers like The

Lord's Prayer in Matthew 6:9–13. We may also read prayers from a book or say spontaneous ones that come from the heart. They can be said in our minds, in a whisper, or out loud.

The exciting part of developing a prayer life is that we can learn to trust God and commit everything to Him, in spite of any problems or challenges we are facing.

Reading and studying the Bible increases our awareness and knowledge about becoming more God-centered and having the desire to please Him. Applying scriptural principles as a pattern for living can make a big difference when it comes to getting the help, guidance, and direction we need to stay on the right path.

There are many Bible verses that have meant a lot to Tom and me. The following verses, listed under topical headings, are examples of Scriptures we have found very helpful and inspiring in our daily walk with God:

Anger

If you are angry, don't sin by nursing your grudge. Don't let the sun go down with you still angry—get over it quickly.

—Ephesians 4:26

A gentle answer turns away wrath, but a harsh word stirs up anger.

—Proverbs 15:1 NIV

Take note of this: Everyone should be quick to listen, slow to speak and slow to become angry, for man's anger does not bring about the righteous life that God desires.

—James 1:19–20 NIV

Comfort

Praise be to the God and Father of our Lord Jesus Christ, the Father of compassion and the God of all comfort, who comforts us in all our troubles, so that we can comfort those in any trouble with the comfort we ourselves have received from God.

—2 Corinthians 1:3–4 NIV

Fear

So do not fear, for I am with you; do not be dismayed, for I am your God. I will strengthen you and help you; I will uphold you with my righteous right hand.

—Isaiah 41:10 NIV

For God hath not given us the spirit of fear; but of power and of love and of a sound mind.

—2 Timothy 1:7 KJV

The Lord is my light and my salvation—whom shall I fear? The Lord is the stronghold of my life—of whom shall I be afraid?

—Psalm 27:1 NIV

Guidance and Direction

I will instruct you (says the Lord) and guide you along the best pathway for your life; I will advise you and watch your progress.

—Psalm 32:8

Trust in the Lord with all your heart and lean not on your own understanding; in all your ways acknowledge him and he will make your paths straight.

—Proverbs 3:5–6 NIV

My sheep listen to my voice; I know them, and they follow me.

—John 10:27 NIV

Healing

A man with leprosy came and knelt before him and said, "Lord, if you are willing, you can make me clean." Jesus reached out his hand and touched the man. "I am willing," he said. "Be clean!" Immediately he was cured of his leprosy.

—Matthew 8:2–3 NIV

Jesus went through all the towns and villages, teaching in their synagogues, preaching the good news of the kingdom and healing every disease and sickness.

—Matthew 9:35 NIV

And Jesus went forth, and saw a great multitude, and was moved with compassion toward them, and he healed their sick.

—Matthew 14:14 KJV

Great crowds came to him bringing the lame, the blind, the crippled, the mute and many others, and laid them at his feet; and he healed them. The people were amazed when they saw the mute speaking, the crippled made well, the lame walking and the blind seeing. And they praised the God of Israel.

—Matthew 15:30–31

Jesus looked at them and said, "With man this is impossible, but not with God; all things are possible with God."

—Mark 10:27 NIV

Hope and Encouragement

Be strong and take heart, all you who hope in the Lord.

—Psalm 31:24 NIV

God is our refuge and strength, an ever-present help in trouble.

—Psalm 46:1 NIV

And let us not get tired of doing what is right, for after a while we will reap a harvest of blessing if we don't get discouraged and give up.

—Galatians 6:9

Let him have all your worries and cares, for he is always thinking about you and watching everything that concerns you.

—1 Peter 5:7

Instructions for Living

Do for others what you want them to do for you . . .

—Matthew 7:12

Stop lying to each other; tell the truth, for we are parts of each other and when we lie to each other we are hurting ourselves. If anyone is stealing he must stop it and begin using those hands of his for honest work so he can give to others in need. Don't use bad language. Say only what is good and helpful to those you are talking to, and what will give them a blessing.

—Ephesians 4:25, 28–29

Get rid of all bitterness, rage and anger, brawling and slander, along with every form of malice. Be kind and compassionate to one another, forgiving each other, just as in Christ, God forgave you.

—Ephesians 4:31–32 NIV

Do everything without complaining or arguing, so that you may become blameless and pure children of God without fault . . .

—Phillipians 2:14–15 NIV

Loving God

Love the Lord your God with all your heart and with all your mind and with all your strength.

—Mark 12:30 NIV

Jesus replied, "If anyone loves me, he will obey my teaching . . ."

—John 14:23 NIV

Loving One Another

My command is this: Love each other as I have loved you.

—John 15:12 NIV

Love your enemies, bless them that curse you, do good to them that hate you, and pray for them which despitefully use you, and persecute you.

—Matthew 5:44 KJV

Love must be sincere. Hate what is evil; cling to what is good. Be devoted to one another in brotherly love. Honor one another above yourselves.

—Romans 12:9–10 NIV

Love is patient, love is kind. It does not envy, it does not boast, it is not proud. It is not rude, it is not self-seeking, it is not easily angered, it keeps no record of wrongs. Love does not delight in evil but rejoices with the truth. It always protects, always trusts, always hopes, always perseveres. Love never fails.

—1 Corinthians 13:4–8

Peace

I am leaving with you a gift – peace of mind and heart! And the peace I give isn't fragile like the peace the world gives. So don't be troubled or afraid.

—John 14:27

The Lord gives strength to his people; the Lord blesses his people with peace.

—Psalm 29:11 NIV

Turn from evil and do good; seek peace and pursue it.

—Psalm 34:14 NIV

Thou wilt keep him in perfect peace, whose mind is stayed on thee: because he trusteth in thee.

—Isaiah 26:3 KJV

Don't worry about anything; instead pray about everything; tell God your needs and don't forget to thank him for his answers. If you do this you will experience God's peace, which is far more wonderful than the human mind can understand. His peace will keep your thoughts and your hearts quiet and at rest as you trust in Christ Jesus.

—Phillipians 4:6–7

Prayer

He shall call upon me, and I will answer him: I will be with him in trouble; I will deliver him, and honor him.

—Psalm 91:15 KJV

Ask and it will be given to you; seek and you will find; knock and the door will be opened to you! For everyone who asks receives; he who seeks finds; and to him who knocks, the door will be opened.

—Matthew 7:7–8 NIV

Rest

My soul finds rest in God alone; my salvation comes from him. He alone is my rock and my salvation; he is my fortress, I will never be shaken.

—Psalm 62:1–2 NIV

Come to me, all you who are weary and burdened, and I will give you rest.

—Matthew 11:28 NIV

Tom and I continue to enjoy reading these and other Scriptures that have enriched our lives. As we continually strive to stay focused on practicing what the Bible teaches, we feel stronger in our relationship with God and each other.

Thank you for taking the time to read *Rescued*. It has been a privilege to share our story with you. God bless you richly. You are special!

Yolanda and Tom Barbagallo

Contact Information

We'd love to hear from you!

You can reach us online at:
rescued.couple@yahoo.com

To order additional copies of this book,
please visit www.redemption-press.com.
Also available on Amazon.com and BarnesandNoble.com
or by calling toll free 1 (844) 273-3336.

CPSIA information can be obtained at www.ICGtesting.com
Printed in the USA
BVOW03s1437100514

352784BV00001B/23/P